WITHDRAWN

COLLEGES
IN CONSORT

*Institutional Cooperation
Through Consortia*

Franklin Patterson

with a Foreword by
Robert C. Wood

COLLEGES IN CONSORT

Jossey-Bass Publishers

San Francisco · Washington · London · 1974

COLLEGES IN CONSORT
Institutional Cooperation Through Consortia
    by Franklin Patterson

Copyright © 1974 by: Jossey-Bass, Inc., Publishers
                 615 Montgomery Street
                 San Francisco, California 94111
                        &
                 Jossey-Bass Limited
                 3 Henrietta Street
                 London WC2E 8LU

Library of Congress Catalogue Card Number LC 73-20964

International Standard Book Number ISBN 0-87589-218-3

Manufactured in the United States of America

JACKET DESIGN BY WILLI BAUM

FIRST EDITION

Code 7418

The Jossey-Bass
Series in Higher Education

FOREWORD

The academic year 1973–1974 is likely to go down as a banner one for talking and writing about public higher education. The Carnegie Commission concluded a six-year venture in self-analysis; the Committee for Economic Development added the perspectives of the business community; and the federal government unleashed a series of analyses and pronouncements. These reports, highly publicized and carefully unveiled, are likely to receive more initial attention than Franklin Patterson's *Colleges in Consort*. However, his carefully researched, tightly reasoned, and action-oriented analysis may well prove to have far more influence on the future of higher education.

While the other studies offer a plethora of self-justification and self-criticism, wring hands, and counsel retreat, Professor Patterson's analysis is realistic in terms of the problems that face collaborative effort in higher education today, but is fundamentally optimistic—an article of faith in the basic integrity of the enterprise.

Based on the results of more than a year of intensive field work, interviews, and analyses, *Colleges in Consort* provides us with the first comprehensive picture of collective efforts for advancing college and university work. With these professional descriptions comes the enlightened and experienced judgment of a leader in academic innovation. The result, not surprisingly, is a carefully constructed picture of consortia activities and a set of major recommendations that if accepted will change the pattern of academic organization. In brisk and precise language, Professor Patterson details efforts toward voluntary cooperation, documents their shortcomings, and proposes how the consortium movement can become truly effective.

His fundamental message is that, with the day of pure autonomy among colleges and universities virtually done, the maintenance of academic freedom in its fundamental sense depends on collaboration and cooperation among institutions that up to now have been substantially independent. As Professor Patterson notes, economic, political, and educational pressures combine to demand modification of the historic pattern of institutional separatism. Witness to this pressure exists in the establishment of state superboards for coordination and the rise in the public sector of systems of institutions, some of which—as in New York and California—involve hundreds of thousands of students.

If these forces are to be dealt with, and constructively, and if the independent genius of American higher education is to be preserved, then universities and colleges must learn to practice effective cooperation. How to do so by providing common services, correlating academic programs, and adjusting academic resources is the subject of *Colleges in Consort*. I commend it to everyone—trustee, administrator, faculty, and student alike—who is concerned with the future of higher education institutions.

Robert C. Wood
President
University of Massachusetts

PREFACE

In the fall of 1971, Harold Howe II, vice-president of The Ford Foundation, suggested to me that it might be useful to take a look at the consortium movement among American colleges and universities. My own experience with a consortium during five years as president of Hampshire College had impressed me with the possibilities and problems of interinstitutional cooperation. I was well aware also that the Carnegie Commission on Higher Education, the Assembly on University Goals and Governance, and other bodies had pointed to the exploration of interinstitutional cooperation as an important task for higher education.

After further talks with Marshall Robinson, deputy vice-president of The Ford Foundation, I agreed to tackle a study of consortia, not as a quantitative survey, but as one interested observer's look at the status, problems, and prospects of cooperative groups of institutions in higher education.

Arrangements were then made to enable me to go about making the study which is reported here. Robert C. Wood, president of the University of Massachusetts, encouraged me to go into the study as an undertaking appropriate to my appointment as Professor of the University, a position concerned with institutional innovation and development. His encouragement was supplemented by support from The Ford Foundation which provided me with the time and assistance to undertake the study.

The result is a modest but hopefully useful examination of the relatively recent movement toward voluntary cooperation among American colleges and universities. I have not intended that this examination would yield up all there is to know about all aspects of all cooperative groups of institutions in the present period. Instead, my purpose has been to establish a general picture of the main outlines and characteristics of the movement, highlight these through concrete examples, and arrive at a provisional assessment, noting strengths, weaknesses, and possible future directions for interinstitutional cooperation.

I employed a methodology which seemed to me to be congenial to this purpose. Because I am not enthusiastic about the species "survey questionnaire," I eschewed its use. Instead, I relied on three other means for arriving at data and insights.

One was documentary. I turned to the reports, financial statements, organizational records, self-studies, and so on that the consortia themselves have prepared; I attempted to correspond with all consortium executive directors in the field; and I examined graduate theses, special monographs, conference reports, and other papers, including the very helpful newsletter about consortia, *The Acquainter,* edited by Lewis D. Patterson, formerly of the Kansas City Regional Council on Higher Education and now of the American Association for Higher Education.

A second means was that of field visits to consortia to talk with executive directors and staff members, observe central office operations, and see participating institutions, their presidents, other administrators, and faculty. Of the more than sixty-five consortia in the country that meet the definition established by Lewis Patterson, I visited twenty-six, representing a cross-section of the movement in terms of geographic regions, types of institutions, and types of consortia. I am grateful to the people who have helped make these visits instructive. I have some confidence in the generalizations presented in this report chiefly because they arose out of direct observation and inquiry in a variety of field sites.

A third means was the use of informed witnesses of the consortium phenomenon. The study owes much to long talks with Lewis D. Patterson, perhaps the best-informed person in the field, North Burn, the able coordinator of Five Colleges, Incorporated, and a number of other professional leaders of the movement. Their depth and breadth of information and their insights born of reflection on extensive direct experience provide a rich resource which I tapped freely and with considerable benefit. At the same time, I reached conclusions independently of their views, for better or worse; and they are in no way responsible or accountable for the strengths or shortcomings of this book. In particular I would like to express my gratitude to the following, whose thoughtful and generous contributions in correspondence and conversation were significant and influential: Henry A. Acres, Charles J. Armstrong, William W. Barnard, Howard R. Bowen, John Brademas, David W. Breneman, Doris P. Bryan, Paul H. Carnell, Earl Cheit, Joseph P. Cosand, Merrimon Cuninggim, Winthrop S. Dakin, Thomas J. Diener, Ian H. Douglas, Philip Driscoll, E. Alden Dunham, Mary H. Ellis, Lawrence E. Fox, Francis C. Gamelin, Robert L. Gluckstern, Morton R. Godine, Samuel B. Gould, Jean D. Grambs, Fritz H. Grupe, Henry Halstead, George W. Hazzard, Mahlon H. Hellerich, Harold L. Hodgkinson, Harold Howe II, Harold F. Johnson, Lynn G. Johnson, James R. Killian, Jr., Robert H. Kroepsch, William J. Lanier, H. Parker Lansdale, Robert E. Leestamper, Douglas W. Lyons, Lillian C. Manley, Sidney P. Marland, Jr., Paul A. Marrotte, Dan M. Martin, Robert H. McCambridge, Robert McCleery, Richard M. Millard, John D. Millett, Richard H. Morgan, Henry W. Munroe, William C. Nelsen, Frederick W. Ness, Ross C. Peavey, Willa B. Player, William G. Pollard, Theodore Provo, Gary H. Quehl, Richard Raeuchle, Marshall Robinson, Arden K. Smith, G. Kerry Smith, Sidney G. Tickton, Dean E. Tollefson, Everette L. Walker, Prince E. Wilson, Richard M. Witter, Herbert Wood, Robert C. Wood, and Thomas M. Woodard.

I wish to acknowledge with all gratitude, too, the careful and imaginative aid given me by Wilson Pile, my assistant. His insights as well as his meticulous culling of data have been of great and continuing help. Thanks go as well to Carol Pope and Margaret Clark for sustaining the study by the important daily tasks of materials organization and manuscript preparation.

    With appreciation for the aid of these and other people, and
thanks to The Ford Foundation and the University of Massachusetts for helping make the study possible, the report remains my
responsibility. To the degree it proves useful, it is because many have
helped; but any inaccuracies or lacks must be laid to my door.

Boston   FRANKLIN PATTERSON
January 1974

CONTENTS

7. What To Do Until Big Brother Comes   117

    Profiles of Consortia   132

    Bibliography   171

    Index   177

COLLEGES
IN CONSORT

Institutional Cooperation
Through Consortia

Chapter 1

HISTORY AND OVERVIEW

In the mid-1960s, James M. Cass, a perceptive observer of American education predicted that "a growing number of colleges and universities, both public and private, both the strong and the less strong, will enter into cooperative programs with neighboring institutions. In this way it will be economically possible for them to offer their students a wider range of special studies and facilities than any one institution could provide alone. In an era in which there will be far more than enough students to go around, the traditional competition between institutions of higher learning will give way to cooperation" (1964, p. 618). At about the same time, in a review of major problems facing colleges and universities, John W. Gardner warned that "we're going to have to learn lessons about planned diversity among institutions and also some hard lessons about cooperation among institutions" with "an attentiveness to the economics of education greater than any we have exhibited in the past" (1965).

1

Such predictions and admonitions seemed to be symptoms of the beginning of a new era in the organization of higher education in the United States. The old pattern of every college or university going it alone, it was thought, would be eroded by the pressure of virtually unlimited needs on limited resources. Every institution, public and private, was facing the fact that its costs were rising faster than its income. In addition, the expansion of knowledge with which higher education was expected to deal was so great and exponential that cooperative relationships seemed necessary for instruction across the range of possibilities to be adequate in quality and variety. It was becoming an article of faith, if not of fact, that in colleges and universities, "the greatest actual need, for the welfare of the whole educational enterprise, is to establish and radically strengthen the cooperative association of diverse institutions in regions or localities, or in special areas of interest" (F. K. Patterson and C. R. Longsworth, 1966, p. 16).

As Eldon L. Johnson observed, in contrast to an earlier day of institutional independence, higher education had "entered a reverse historical phase which seems to embrace interinstitutional coordination and cooperation as a necessary step for completeness" (1967, p. 341).

On first examination, the facts seem to bear out the accuracy of such statements. By the mid-sixties, it was possible for Raymond Moore to identify 1,017 formal cooperative arrangements in American higher education, in which more than 1,500 institutions were participating. Moore's inventory listed 637 bilateral arrangements, 596 arrangements operative without an independent budget, and a variety of other mechanisms (1968). Of these arrangements, the largest number involved only graduate education. Moore's inventory was useful in suggesting the extent to which colleges and universities had found it advisable to work together, but suffered from being too inclusive and indiscriminate.

In 1967 Lewis D. Patterson, then of the Kansas City Regional Council for Higher Education, undertook a more discriminating inventory, concentrating on consortia which had some commonality because they met similar standards. Thirty-one consortia were identified as meeting five specific criteria: (1) a voluntary formal organization, (2) three or more member institutions, (3) multiacademic programs, (4) at least one full-time professional to administer consortium programs, and (5) a required annual contribution or other tangible evidence of the long-term commitment of member institutions (1970, p. 3). Patterson's initiative marked a significant step toward clarifying and understanding the consortium movement. In June 1967 he wrote to the directors of sixteen of these consortia and invited an exchange of information. The response to his invitation was immediate and enthusiastic, beginning a process of continuing interaction and communication among staff people and others concerned with the movement. Between 1967 and 1970 eight national meetings of consortia personnel were held, and joint committees were formed to represent the interests of interinstitutional cooperation nationally. Within the Kansas City Regional Council for Higher Education (KCRCHE) Patterson established an informal consortium information center and acted as its archivist and editor. He began a mimeographed bulletin, *The Acquainter: An International Newsletter for Academic Consortia,* and an annual listing, the *Consortium Directory: Voluntary Academic Cooperative Arrangements in Higher Education,* which he has continued since moving to the American Association for Higher Education.

The fifth edition of Patterson's *Directory,* in 1971, listed sixty-six groupings, involving 684 institutions of which 662 were institutions of higher education, an increase of 113 percent over the thirty-one four years earlier. The sixth *Directory* in 1973 listed eighty consortia involving 797 institutions, 774 of them in higher education—an increase of 21 percent since the fifth edition. Patterson found that approximately twelve new consortia meeting his criteria were being established each year, with an attrition rate of approximately one per year.

Certainly one of the most impressive facts about the consortium movement is its relative recency. Considering only consortia that meet the five standards established by Patterson, and admittedly disregarding other cooperative groups within higher education, between 1925 and 1965 nineteen consortia were established: four by 1948, five more by 1958, and an additional ten by 1965. In the next five years, from 1965 to 1970, thirty-two more came into being (L. Patterson, 1970, p. 1). As of the present writing, over one-half of today's consortia have been organized in the past five years.

Whatever their causes, and no matter how substantial they are, the rapidly increasing number of consortia and other interinstitutional cooperative arrangements constitutes a notable phenomenon in American higher education. It flies directly in the face of the historic pattern of institutional isolationism and independence which has dominated higher education until the present time. This movement constitutes something new in education: at the very least, a rhetorical and nominal commitment to cooperation, where before had existed a kind of friendly anarchy among colleges and universities.

As nearly as I can tell, however, neither of the two principal doctrines or ideological impulses that inform the consortium movement is yet fully fulfilled in any part of the movement. Indeed, one can question whether the commitments that they require for fulfillment will ever be forthcoming.

The first of these doctrines is that through cooperation the academic programs available to students can be substantially enriched and made more diverse. This doctrine is realized only on a modest scale even among the best of the consortia, and it would not be accurate to say that enrichment of academic programs has yet been generally achieved by the consortium movement. Indeed, when it comes to academic matters, the faculties at institutions, no matter how radical they may be in social and political protest, turn out to be conservative in protecting what they regard as their vested institutional interests. No one in the consortium movement can be faulted for excessive zeal in promoting the cooperative interinstitutional planning of academic programs. Instead, institutional territoriality tends to prevail, making those concerned appear more willing to adhere to what President John Silber of Boston University calls the "principle of redundancy" than to the idea of planned complementarity.

The second doctrine, that of economic gains through cooperation, turns out to be even more a matter of shadow than substance, despite the fact that the doctrine of economy seems to have self-evident validity to many observers. "The growth of interinstitutional cooperation," Lewis Patterson has written, ". . . testifies to the belief that survival and viability will be found through group affiliation" (1970, p. 1). And in discussing avenues to effective use of resources in colleges and universities, the Carnegie Commission on Higher Education asserted that "significant economies can be achieved through consortium agreements and other forms of inter-institutional cooperation. . . ." Largely on the basis of economic arguments, the Commission recommended "the development and strengthening of consortia in higher education" and urged "increased cooperation and sharing of facilities by public and private institutions . . . in all states" (1972, pp. 127–128). There is enough evidence in the experience of consortia to warrant these hopes that interinstitutional cooperation can permit financial economies, or, at any rate, the wiser, more effective use of resources than individual institutions can conduct alone. At the same time, the Carnegie Commission itself notes that "a good many of the consortia are paper arrangements with little significance in practice," and that there is "serious resistance in colleges and universities to any departure from the traditional goal of independent development of the resources of each institution" (1972, p. 128).

In point of fact, few hard-nosed joint decisions are yet being made within consortia about avoiding redundancy in new physical plant or achieving cooperative economies in purchasing, admissions, use of educational technology, or the like. A number of presidents are at least rhetorically committed to cooperation, but their substantive commitment remains to be really tested; and it is clear that whatever their commitment, it tends to outrun that of their faculties and trustees.

Subsequent sections of this report will present in more detail the variety of form and experience within the consortium movement, the fundamental economic questions that are raised by the movement, the strengths and weaknesses of academic cooperation, and the alternatives which colleges and universities need to consider in connection with interinstitutional cooperation. In overview here, however, and later in more detail, the accomplishment of the movement in light of its promise will prove to be a mixed picture.

The consortium movement, as defined in this report, began slowly nearly forty years ago. Although the Carnegie Commission

refers to them as a formal federation rather than a consortium, The
Claremont Colleges are considered by most observers to have begun
the movement in the United States in 1925 when James A. Blais-
dell, president of Pomona College, created a plan reminiscent of
Oxford to establish a small group of colleges around Pomona, with
a library and other facilities which they might use in common. The
first edition in this cluster was The Claremont Graduate School,
followed over the next several decades by Scripps College, Claremont Men's College, Harvey Mudd College, and Pitzer College.

In 1929, four years after the founding of The Claremont
Colleges, the Atlanta University Center was begun in Georgia by
agreements among Atlanta University, Morehouse, and Spelman
Colleges. Later, Clark College, the Interdenominational Theological
Center, and Morris Brown College entered into working arrangements with the Center, and in 1964 they finally joined under a new
charter.

The movement proceeded slowly after these beginnings in
Claremont and Atlanta. As noted earlier, the main pickup in momentum began in the early 1960s, as colleges and universities began to feel the full brunt of the greatest enrollment rise in the history
of American higher education, coupled with economic inflation and
the knowledge explosion.

By 1962, the momentum was sufficiently strong, and the
awareness of common developmental problems sufficiently great,
that a conference on college and university interinstitutional cooperation was held at Princeton, sponsored by one consortia, the
College Center of the Finger Lakes (ccfl), and supported by The
Ford Foundation, the Corning Glass Works Foundation, and
Arthur A. Houghton, Jr. It brought together staff leaders of then-
existing consortia with other educators and foundation representatives; and was in many ways a milestone, marking the beginning of
a serious professional dialogue about the movement at a more or
less national level. The Princeton discussions, summarized in published proceedings, set forth thirty-two areas of possible cooperation,
which pretty well covered the range of collaborative considerations
that would come before higher education and anticipated the more
frequent appearance of literature on cooperation later in the decade
(Wittich, 1962).

In 1965, the United States Congress endorsed interinstitutional cooperation as a means for improving higher education in the nation. Title III of the Higher Education Act of 1965 (P.L. 89-329) provided support for "cooperative arrangements" among "developing institutions." Colleges judged to be "struggling for survival" and "isolated from the main currents of academic life" would qualify to receive Title III funds for cooperative efforts to improve their position; and a substantial number of consortia came into being under the stimulus of Title III.

This national intervention has in several cases been supplemented at the state level. New York and Connecticut, for example, have enacted legislation to encourage interinstitutional cooperation. In New York, the Bundy Committee (the Governor's Select Committee on Aid to Private Higher Education) urged state appropriation of a million dollars to stimulate cooperation among colleges and universities.

By the time the College Center of the Finger Lakes sponsored a second major conference in 1969, the number of consortia had doubled in comparison with that in 1962. The 1969 conference reflected the rapid growth of the movement through a natural preoccupation with organizational concerns: Its conferees were occupied with questions of organizational structure, intraconsortium relationships, the executive director's role, cooperative program development, and ways to finance interinstitutional cooperation (Burnett, 1970).

As the number of Title III and non-Title III consortia multiplied, and more meetings and conferences were held, the literature of the movement burgeoned swiftly. By January, 1971, Lewis D. Patterson required thirty-six pages to list articles, theses, and other papers in a *Comprehensive Bibliography on Interinstitutional Cooperation with Special Emphasis on Voluntary Academic Consortia in Higher Education* (1971c). By the early 1970's, then, the consortium movement was sizeable—at least in terms of the literature about it, the number of institutions involved, and the hopes raised for its usefulness.

The consortium movement arose out of a context of factors whose reality could not be questioned. The day of the wholly autonomous institution was coming to an end. The approach of post-

industrial society, in Daniel Bell's sense, presented higher education
with complex social and educational demands and financial constraints that made it increasingly difficult for institutions to go it
alone. For a large number of private institutions, including such
hitherto invulnerable giants as Columbia and Penn, the question
was becoming one of survival itself. The passage of the Higher Education Act of 1972, authorizing some nineteen billion dollars of
federal support for colleges and universities, signaled a turning point
in federal aid to higher education which might speak to the needs of
institutions and students more adequately. But it was not likely that
the public, through government or gift, would provide progressively
more massive subsidy to allow each institution to remain in splendid
isolation, trying to offer education of high quality all across the
board. It seemed increasingly clear that no matter how austere and
efficient internal management could be made, nor how friendly the
federal government might be to their cause, few if any colleges and
universities would be able to stand wholly alone much longer.

The new era in the organization of higher education appears
likely to bring with it more joint planning and collaboration among
institutions than we have been used to. Unrealistically oversimplified, some educators think the issue is whether this will happen by
involuntary coordination, directed by state and national government, or through cooperation, voluntarily entered into by public
and private institutions. Actually, both more coordination and more
cooperation are likely. By the end of the century, increasing dependence on governmental support—even by today's richest institutions
—will have brought with it a new kind of accountability and, with
it, more coordination from outside. A realistic question is whether
voluntary cooperation can take hold and work well enough to miti-
gate some of the thrust toward externally directed coordination.

Ideally, if cooperation adequate to academic and economic
needs could be established through voluntary consortia, the new era
might follow a pattern of interinstitutional self-government more
than one patterned by the requirements of federal and state accountability. Under voluntary cooperation, decisions about complementary educational missions, faculty development and support,
and costly installations would be made by those most directly involved, acting through self-governing groups of institutions. But it

is certainly not clear yet whether voluntary consortia will be able to achieve genuine and significant cooperation in any way adequate to the circumstances, or soon enough. The old pattern of institutional autonomy dies hard.

In sum, while interinstitutional cooperation of a strong kind is needed, and while promising instances of what might be achieved through consortia are easy to come by, the movement at this point is insubstantial and shaky. The fundamental question to which interested parties will have to address themselves is twofold: Is there sufficient promise in existing consortia to justify a belief that they can be made adequately effective, and, if so, what are the most practical ways to make the movement really move? The following discussion of the diversity and types of consortia, their economics, their governance and leadership, their program strengths and weaknesses, and their future possibilities aim at responding to this twofold question.

Chapter 2

A PROVISIONAL TYPOLOGY

Consortia which have the five characteristics in common identified by Lewis Patterson exhibit so much other diversity that it is difficult indeed to classify them. The typology that I suggest in the following discussion is therefore provisional and general.

A quick review of the fifty-five active consortia on which this study has detailed information suggests some of their diversity. Thirty-two of them involve public institutions of higher education in at least a nominal way. Only two exclude private institutions, and both of these appear to be in some measure paper organizations. The fifty-five vary considerably in number of members. The smallest has three member institutions; the largest has fifty-four.

Seven of the fifty-five consortia are organized to provide teacher preparation in urban areas, featuring in-service, undergraduate, and graduate training. Ten of the fifty-five cooperate to provide programs of environmental studies. Eleven cooperatively offer year-long off-campus programs off-campus; some of them abroad, others in urban service and studies and other fields.

Twenty-six of the fifty-five permit cross-registration by students among their member institutions, twenty-four specifically do not do so; and two are developing a program of cross-registration. Six feature joint admissions programs, and three have cooperative admissions programs limited to specific categories of potential scholars. Fifteen have joint committees on admission; twenty have some sort of interinstitutional departmental committees; and nineteen have interinstitutional administrative committees below the presidential level. Eleven publish a joint calendar; fifteen are involved in some species of shared faculty program; nineteen share in joint cultural programs of one kind or another; twelve offer visiting lecturer programs; and twenty offer some form of cooperative support for faculty research.

In the whole group of fifty-five, twenty-six offer one or another kind of shared library program, the most common being cross-cataloguing and a system of interlibrary lending. There is some joint purchasing of books, and there are eleven central journal deposits and six joint film libraries. Eight share computer facilities in various ways; one has a complex and well-used telephone networking system; and one has a sophisticated but highly practical microwave television network.

Among these fifty-five consortia, public institutions seem less involved and less interested in cooperative efforts than do the private institutions. The University of New Hampshire, for example, appears significantly less active in the New Hampshire College and University Council than are the Council's private institutions; and the two state universities in Greensboro, North Carolina, have expressed no active interest in becoming involved in the Greensboro Tri-College Consortium. With few exceptions public universities and colleges do not appear to be taking the lead and rarely maintain even a middle-range role in any of the consortia.

Of the fifty-five, only thirteen involve community or junior colleges. These institutions appear to have particular problems with cooperative arrangements and service consortia. Four-year colleges and universities have shown little imagination, as have the two-year community and junior colleges themselves, in working out ways by which the two-year colleges can be productively related to other institutions in a consortium. The few creative exceptions include the Worcester Consortium for Higher Education which actively includes two private junior colleges and one public community college, and the College Center of the Finger Lakes. In the latter case, Cazenovia College, a private junior college, has worked out arrangements with the three four-year colleges which make up the balance of the consortium so that every "good standing" graduate of Cazenovia is guaranteed acceptance by one of the other three member institutions. The effect is that Cazenovia, without the cost of an upper division, assures upper division benefits to its students. Cazenovia students are able, for instance, to take a junior year abroad under the auspices of their new home campus without ever having spent a day there. Since many junior and community college graduates encounter transfer problems and a growing number of four-year private colleges are having problems recruiting students, this kind of arrangement in the College Center of the Finger Lakes suggests a possible new departure in cooperative activities, setting up two-year institutions as feeders into troubled four-year colleges.

In terms of size, my own sense is that it is difficult indeed for a cooperative effort to be very successful with more than seven or eight member institutions. Cooperative effort involving an institution intensely will by its very nature involve conflict and compromise, and the larger the number of institutions involved, the more diluted (or disputed) the eventual product is likely to be. Where a consortium exists to provide service to member institutions, bigness appears to lead to fragmentation among members in terms of their relative degree of interest in its services. An example is the New Hampshire College and University Council, with eleven members and obvious fragmentation within its membership. The University of New Hampshire sits off to one side in splendid isolation, as does Colby Junior College on another. The two New Hampshire state colleges form a third subset. An additional fragmentation is between those institutions which are Catholic and those which are not.

A movement toward more cohesiveness and fewer members in the College Center of the Finger Lakes is worth noting in this connection. CCFL, which included nine member institutions at one point, has undergone substantial trimming and reorganization in the recent past and at present is down to a core membership of four institutions. These four appear to be in active, productive cooperation with each other and are selling certain services to the five former member institutions plus any other institution which may desire such assistance.

Expansion, then, seems to be a weakening influence in consortium experience. One might reasonably postulate about size that the larger the number of member institutions, the more ambiguous the consortium; the greater the geographic area covered, the more ambiguous the consortium; and the greater the range in higher educational levels (two-year, four-year, university level), the more ambiguous the consortium.

Yet it is equally clear that consortia can be too small. A three-member consortium becomes at best a bilateral agreement when one institution withdraws, as happened with the Consortium of Northern New England in 1972. In this particular case, three highly selective private liberal arts colleges—Bates, Bowdoin, and Colby—established the consortium in 1971 to share off-campus programs, including a summer course on the geology of Maine, a semester in mammalia at the Jackson Laboratory in Bar Harbor, a Washington semester at American University, and international studies coordinated through the Central Pennsylvania Consortium. Despite the efforts of its energetic director, Ian Douglas, the consortium was never able to move "on campus" to attempt real interinstitutional cooperation. Its failure was in part due to change of presidents at one of the member institutions.

In the smaller consortium the importance of presidential commitment is proportionately large, and most cannot survive a negative shift by any member institution. As Arden Smith of the Central Pennsylvania Consortium pointed out (1973): "First, while a smaller consortium may be more effective, perhaps three members may be just too small. Second, and perhaps more important, unless the presidents really mean it when they say they want to cooperate, even at doing the 'easy things,' one might as well forget the whole business."

The healthiest consortia seem to me to be those that share two basic characteristics: they have a manageable number of member institutions, and clear-cut, agreed-upon goals and functions.

Three such consortia that come to mind as examples are the United
Independent Colleges of Art (UICA), the Christian College Consortium, and The Association for Graduate Education and Research
(TAGER). UICA, a national consortium of colleges of art, has a limited
number of members and very specific functions, particularly with
regard to admissions. The Christian College Consortium, also national, focuses specifically on building "a university system of Christian colleges." TAGER links a group of institutions in the Dallas-
Fort Worth area by television interconnection for shared instruction,
principally in the fields of technology and science.

The variety of characteristics mentioned above suggests how
difficult it is to categorize consortia. In a sense, a consortium of
colleges or universities by nature has to be unique, a vehicle specified by the needs, interests, and opportunities peculiar to the institutions that become associated. Even so, there are constraining
factors that tend to produce some uniformities and a rough kind of
typology in the movement. Among these constraints are the limited
choice of possible consortium missions, in which only a few basic
options exist; the similar financial realities with which nearly all
private colleges must contend; the federal guidelines and incentives
of Title III, later legislation, and the United States Office of Education; and the not very great degree to which most institutions are
willing to relinquish sovereignty. These and other influences combine to make it possible to sort out consortia in at least a provisional
way, and a number of efforts to do so have occurred in the past
decade. (Andrews, 1964; Donovan, 1964; L. Patterson, 1970; Wilson, 1965). The tripartite typology suggested here—cooperative,
service, and Title III consortia—is probably no more perfect than
those put forth by others, but it seems to me to grow naturally out
of these data.

Cooperative Consortia. From the beginning of the movement in 1925, the consortia which have attracted the most public
attention and general recognition have been ones whose intentions
involved, in greater or lesser degree, joint academic planning and
cooperative academic programs. In at least a nominal sense, the
Claremont colleges set a general mode or standard for a number of
consortia which were to come later. The Claremont system itself has
not been adopted widely, but its apparent commitment to interac-

tion among its colleges—its pooling and sharing of certain significant resources, its establishment of some planned differentiation of mission among its members—made it a useful first example and point of reference. When the idea of a group of colleges associating for academic purposes came up in the conversation of professors or presidents elsewhere, Claremont was likely to be mentioned.

Today, certain consortia reflect characteristics of academic cooperation enough to warrant our regarding them as being in a distinct category. Many, like the Greensboro Tri-College Consortium, depend heavily on Title III funding. A few others do not. In a number of ways the most fully developed example of a voluntary cooperative consortium is Five Colleges, Incorporated, in the Connecticut River Valley of western Massachusetts. Not as old as the consortia at Claremont and at Atlanta, Five Colleges, Incorporated is well established enough to reveal some of the strengths and weaknesses of the cooperative consortium.

Informal cooperation among Amherst, Mount Holyoke, Smith, and the University of Massachusetts has a long history. The first formal connection was made in 1951, with the establishment of the Hampshire Inter-Library Center, a cooperative depository for infrequently used books and periodicals of importance to the faculty and students of the four institutions. In 1956, under a Ford Foundation grant, a committee of faculty from the four institutions strongly recommended further cooperative programs. It seemed wasteful for each institution to seek competitive eminence in such specialized fields as astronomy, advanced Russian, Asian languages, the history of science, and the like. Duplication of small courses and costly research and teaching equipment appeared patently uneconomical. After 1956, formal and informal cooperation among the four institutions increasingly became more than talk. The Ford Foundation supported further planning and a new experimenting undergraduate college was projected by an interinstitutional committee of faculty. This institution was intended by its designers to be deliberately dependent on cooperation with its older sisters. The "New College Plan" eventually resulted in the chartering of Hampshire College in 1965, and the fifth institution of the consortium began active operation in 1970.

During the 1960's, the institutions edged steadily towards a formal collective organization. At the beginning of the decade they cooperated rather casually under a committee of the presidents, assisted by a faculty member as a part-time coordinator. After the chartering of Hampshire College in 1965, the institutions drew together more closely as members of a new corporate body, Five Colleges, Incorporated, governed by a board made up of the five presidents; and in 1967, North Burn, previously vice-president of Mills College, was appointed as the first full-time Five College Coordinator.

The presidents gave increasing consideration to Five College development as a basic way of forwarding the educational missions of their own institutions. Their academic deans, business officers, librarians, department chairmen, and others were called upon to take initiative in cooperative planning as a regular activity. A Long-Range Planning Committee of fifteen persons (five academic deans, five senior professors, and five chief business officers), during a hard year of work, laid out future goals and means for the complex in *Five College Cooperation: Directions for the Future* (1969)—perhaps the best planning document the consortium movement has yet produced.

For the past two years, Five College presidents have been meeting far from casually, once each month. Current examples of Five College cooperation, most of which bear directly on academic planning, include student interchange, faculty interchange, joint academic programs, academic coordination, and certain specialized activities:

Students at one college can, without charge, enroll in courses at the other colleges. In 1971–72 there were more than 4,500 semester course interchange enrollments. An hourly Five College bus system among the colleges makes transportation for such interchange enrollment and other purposes relatively easy.

Professors on one campus often teach a course on another. Some receive joint appointments; others, as among the philosophy departments in the academic year 1972–73, trade teaching assignments to vary their experience. All letters appointing new faculty in institutions of the consortium now specify that, under appropriate arrangements, teaching at another of the Five Colleges is considered a normal duty.

Joint academic programs range from the Five College Black

Studies Program to the Five College Department of Astronomy. Currently, eight Five College cooperative Ph.D. programs exist, including German, philosophy, chemistry, biology, in addition to astronomy and other fields.

Academic coordination is maintained by the five principal academic officers meeting twice a month with North Burn. Currently, the academic deans are reviewing all departments in the Five Colleges to eliminate unnecessary duplication of courses and achieve further joint offerings. In the academic year 1971–72, the deans succeeded in placing all five institutions on a common yearly schedule, permitting easier interchange in the January term as well as in both regular semesters.

Other activities include Five College radio, WFCR-FM, an excellent public broadcasting station; faculty seminars in a number of disciplines; low-rate charter flights to Europe; an interlibrary loan system; an active Five College Student Coordinating Board; a Five College Calendar of Events; a common index of courses in the five institutions; a joint studio for electronic music; and much else. The story of Five Colleges is one of many strengths, with more very probable. The Five Colleges are undoubtedly better educationally for being together than they would be alone; at least rapidly rising student interchange is testimony that the customers think so. Of the four private institutions, Smith and Mount Holyoke are women's colleges, Amherst is a men's college, and Hampshire is coeducational. All four are residential; their enrollment ranging from one thousand at Hampshire to twenty-four hundred at Smith. The University of Massachusetts at Amherst is also principally residential, with a total undergraduate-graduate enrollment approaching twenty-two thousand. All five campuses are relatively close to each other, separated by an average distance of less than seven miles. Together they constitute a unique public-private cluster, with a diverse student population, strong faculty, excellent physical facilities, major library resources, a tradition of good undergraduate teaching, and through the University, emerging high quality at the graduate level. In many ways, Five Colleges is one of the strongest and most interesting consortia in the country. Taken together, the five institutions in the complex look like something new and potentially important in American higher education. The complex pro-

vides an extraordinarily wide range of educational opportunity
through course work and other means, and visibly underlines the
potential advantages of academic cooperation among public and
private institutions.

At the same time, it would be misleading to suggest that
Five Colleges, Incorporated has achieved perfection in cooperation.
Many faculty members and many students in the complex are relatively untouched by the possible benefits of interinstitutional cooperation. While it is true that Five Colleges, Incorporated appears
to be reaching more and more towards planned complementarity in
academic programming, it is equally true that the separate faculties
and administrations continue to guard their institutional autonomy
with some zeal, and that institutional administrations and trustees
have not yet substantially come to grips with the problem of pre-
venting redundancy in capital expenditures and many other matters.

Service Consortia. A second category of consortium utilizes
cooperation principally to provide its constituent institutions with
one or more services. These services may or may not be academic in
nature; the key fact about these consortia is that they exist to serve
their member colleges and universities.

The service consortium is likely to make comparatively few
demands on member institutions for the kind of cooperative planning and academic coordination that typifies the cooperative consortium. I have identified three principal subcategories of service
consortia: single-purpose, federal research, and multipurpose.

A good example of the single-purpose service consortium is
The Marine Science Consortium, Incorporated. In 1965 the chairmen of the science departments of all Pennsylvania state colleges met
to locate and operate a cooperative marine station. These efforts
led to the incorporation of the Marine Science Consortium in the
spring of 1971 as "a nonprofit corporation dedicated to promote
teaching and research in the marine sciences" (Frederick and Oostdam, 1972). Through its administrative center at Millersville State
College in Millersville, Pennsylvania, the consortium operates the
Delaware Bay Marine Science Center at Lewes, Delaware, and the
Wallops Island Marine Science Center at Wallops Island, Virginia.
The present membership of thirteen institutions includes nine Pennsylvania state colleges, Pennsylvania State University, Indiana Uni-

versity of Pennsylvania, West Virginia University, and the Catholic University of America in Washington, D.C.

In its Letter of Agreement, the membership stated the consortium's purpose to: "(a) Promote and encourage teaching in the Marine Sciences on the graduate and undergraduate levels. (b) Promote and encourage pure and applied research in the Marine Sciences. (c) Promote the establishment and operation of field stations to be known as Marine Science Centers to aid in teaching and research in a Marine environment. (d) Encourage and promote dialogue among those interested in Marine Science through meetings and seminars" (Frederick and Oostdam, 1972, pp. 124–125). The consortium carries out a number of programs, financed in roughly equal shares by membership fees, student fees, grants, and contracts. Among the principal activities are a six-week summer program for high school students and undergraduate courses in oceanography and related fields offered by and for the member institutions. These programs are supplemented by an impressive array of equipment, headed by the ninety-foot research vessel, *Annandale,* and including at least five other substantial vessels, three buildings at Delaware Bay, eight buildings at Wallops Island, and twenty-two "Operation Staff" positions.

Single-purpose service consortia like the Marine Science Consortium are certainly conveniences for their membership. The institutions are able to respond to a particular demand—usually environmentally oriented—with a minimum of strain and change on the home campus. It is unlikely such a consortium would ever become multi-purpose. Its form, content, organization, and assets are all centered to one end. Such a consortium is, in essence, a jointly-owned service, used to the degree that its members see fit.

Another subcategory of service consortia is the federal research consortium. These consortia do not meet Lewis Patterson's criteria in that they do not necessarily have a formal organization and they do not require annual contributions or other tangible evidence of long-term commitment. Examples include the Eisenhower Consortium for Western Forestry Research and the Oak Ridge Associated Universities.

The Eisenhower Consortium, founded in the spring of 1972, has a membership composed of nine state universities in Arizona,

Colorado, New Mexico, Texas, and Wyoming and the United States Forest Service Rocky Mountain Forest and Range Experiment Station in Fort Collins, Colorado. In the statement issued at the consortium's creation it was described as "an organization to combine and coordinate the research efforts of interested educational institutions and the Forest Service to solve the problems of man and his interactions with the environment." Its functions are to "select problems, formulate research programs, solicit research proposals to implement these programs, and provide the machinery through which Forest Service research grants are made to universities." The Forest Service agreed to provide funds for the consortium, half for Forest Service in-house research programs and half as grants to participating universities for studies selected by the executive committee (*Forest and Range,* 1972).

Oak Ridge Associated Universities (1971) describes itself as:

> a private, nonprofit corporation sponsored by forty-one colleges and universities in the South, the Association was chartered in the State of Tennessee in 1946 and operated for its first 20 years as the Oak Ridge Institute of Nuclear Studies. The pioneer among corporate university management groups of its type in the United States, ORAU conducts programs of education, information, research, and human resource development under contract with the United States Atomic Energy Commission and on behalf of the AEC and other governmental and private organizations.

ORAU has no rigid formal organization in the sense that any institution in its geographic region may join by signifying its desire to do so, with no costs and no direct benefits except for the honor of having its seal affixed to the lobby wall of the spacious ORAU building at Oak Ridge. This particular consortium serves as a regional vehicle for AEC research and extension funding. Its projects range from "The Atomic World"—a fleet of twenty-three mobile demonstration units highlighting peaceful applications of atomic energy, funded in part by thirty-five utility companies—to fellowships in nuclear science and engineering, environmental courses, nuclear medicine research, and a number of manpower training projects.

These and other single-purpose and federal research consortia, such as the National Center for Atmospheric Research and the Argonne Laboratories, are intentionally omitted from further analysis in this report since they fail to meet its overriding criterion: they are not examples of efforts to achieve broad-gauge interinstitutional cooperation. In addition, federal research consortia have little or nothing to do with institutions *per se*—they deal with interested faculty who may or may not be connected with the so-called "membership."

The third subcategory, the multipurpose service consortium, more clearly meet the criteria established by Lewis Patterson, and, to a certain degree, those of this report. It is likely to provide an array of programs to member colleges which they might not be able to conduct alone or as economically on their own. In return, the participating institutions usually provide the consortium structure with financial support through a basic annual assessment coupled with a schedule of fees for participation in individual programs.

The Associated Colleges of the Midwest (ACM) provides a useful example of a multipurpose service consortium. Headquartered in the Newberry Library in Chicago, ACM is a consortium of twelve coeducational liberal arts colleges with almost completely undergraduate enrollments, geographically scattered through Illinois, Wisconsin, Minnesota, Iowa, and Colorado: Beloit, Carleton, Coe, Colorado, Cornell, Grinnell, Knox, Macalester, Monmouth, Ripon, and St. Olaf Colleges, and Lawrence University. With actual beginnings in the late 1950s, ACM was incorporated in Illinois in 1963. Its basic purpose is to:

> carry on activities which will enrich the programs of each of our twelve ACM colleges—activities which probably could not be carried on by one college alone, or for some reason are too specialized to be accomplished on a single campus. Most of these programs require a locale different from those of any of our twelve campuses. Although a single program should be attractive to a majority of ACM colleges it need not be participated in by all of them. ACM faculty, administrative officers and students are consulted frequently during the planning and development of each of our programs. They and the ACM staff supervise the ongoing activities of each of these programs after adoption by the colleges [ACM, 1970, p. 1].

ACM chooses to break its programs down into two types: academic and service. In reality, both of these types constitute what one may regard as services to the participating institutions, since the "academic" programs in a very real way constitute a service curriculum supplied to the participating colleges. These academic service programs provide off-campus experiences for students in an impressive range of study possibilities: Arabic Studies; Costa Rican Development Studies; East Asian Studies; India Studies; Urban Studies; Urban Teaching; Argonne Semester; Introductory Geology in the Rocky Mountains; Wilderness Field Station; Newberry Library Seminar; New York Arts; and The Arts of London and Florence. The range and richness of the ACM "service" programs also are notable. These include most significantly the ACM periodical bank and service library, the Single Application Method (SAM) for joint admissions and student recruitment to the twelve colleges, and the jointly operated Washington, D.C. office representing all twelve institutions.

The basic membership fee for institutions in ACM currently is thirteen thousand dollars per annum plus one dollar per annum for each student at each institution. Fundamentally, these contributions pay for the Chicago and Washington office operations.

At this writing, ACM lacks interinstitutional academic planning and programing of the kind emerging in Five Colleges, Incorporated. There are no continuing or short-term instrumentalities for long-range planning of cooperative educational programs, and there is no interchange enrollment of students from campus to campus. Dan M. Martin, who became president of ACM in August 1971, acknowledges this fact and hopes to create a council of academic deans which might meet several times a year. Dr. Martin also hopes to have business officers meet on a similar basis. He is emphatic in saying that he does not want ACM simply to be a coordinator of off-campus special programs, but it is not yet clear in his administration how or whether ACM will move from being a service consortium to something more. While its member colleges are more or less similar, they are spread over a very wide territory, and it may be that service is the only appropriate function of their association. In any case, the services that ACM renders are evidently worthwhile.

But both the worthwhileness and the shakiness of some of

these consortium services is illustrated by the ACM periodical bank centrally located at the ACM offices in the Newberry Library. Funded until now by sizable National Science Foundation support, the periodical bank offers three types of services: (1) regular photo-copy service, whereby the bank can provide copies of articles from current or back-file issues of the two thousand periodicals in its holdings which were selected to supplement the basic subscriptions held by the libraries of the twelve member colleges; (2) outside photocopy service, by which the bank provides copies of articles from periodicals not in the bank collection but held by a major re-search library in the Chicago area; and (3) currently runs a photo-copy service, providing copies of the tables of contents of current periodicals to which the bank subscribes. The periodical bank is used with reasonable frequency by ACM member institutions and by other colleges that belong to the bank as associate members. Its operation is efficient and would seem to be a sensible way of strengthening the library resources of small colleges through a cen-tral service. Yet the periodical bank is in perilous condition because its National Science Foundation support is running out and there are no new revenues in sight. Its operation is not paid for by the dues of the constituent colleges, and it is currently possible to have the bank only because of outside support.

ACM is probably one of the best of the service consortia. Its usefulness seems clear, as do its limits. The fundamental current problem it faces is probably characteristic of the service consortia generally: its inability to operate some of its services without either continuing outside subsidy or substantially increased support by the member institutions.

Title III Consortia. How hard it is to generalize about and categorize consortia is made plain by the fact that neither of the two categories thus far described is at all airtight. Cooperative con-sortia are likely to have some service functions, and service con-sortia may verge into interinstitutional academic programs. Both kinds may, at the institutional level, be recipients of Title III funding.

No other single factor, including foundation support, has had as heavy an influence on the consortium movement as has Title III of the Higher Education Act of 1965. This legislation, as noted earlier, greatly accentuated the momentum towards the formation

of consortia during the latter part of the 1960s. Through the provisions of this Title, two-year and four-year colleges which were
"struggling for survival" and "isolated from the main currents of
academic life" were to be given financial aid to try to improve
themselves through cooperation with other institutions. In the
preparation of the legislation, the principal intention was to backstop predominantly black colleges and community colleges, but, as
Father William G. Kelly has pointed out (n.d., p. 3), the term
developing institution used in the legislation easily came to embrace other types of colleges and universities.

The Division of College Support, Bureau of Higher Education, U.S. Office of Education, left the issue open and invited colleges and universities interested in support to justify their claim to
be "developing institutions." On the basis of these justifications,
funding patterns were established in the years after 1965, and this
rough picture has emerged of what a developing institution funded
under Title III looks like: (1) a two-year or four-year institution,
which has been in existence five or more years and has regional accreditation or is in correspondent status with the regional association, or is making "reasonable progress toward accreditation" or
preaccreditation status; (2) a college which is weaker than a
strongly established institution, struggling for academic quality, encountering hard economic difficulties, in need of administrative
strengthening, and confronted with problems of survival "as a result
of economic and social changes beyond its control"; (3) a college
which evidences a desire to improve and which shows potential and
progress towards the realization of its goals; (4) a college which
presents a feasible plan for meeting its fundamental needs through
cooperative arrangements with other colleges or agencies, or both;
and (5) a college which by necessity or desire or both serves the
needs of low-income students (Kelly, n.d., p. 4).

Among institutions funded under Title III two salient statistical facts tend to show up: they have a greater than normal proportion of low-income students, and they tend to have substandard
resources, particularly in terms of library resources. Because of their
relatively high proportion of students from low-income or minority-
group backgrounds, and a higher than normal proportion of entering freshmen from the lowest quartile ranking in high school, they

often show a special need for remedial and compensatory programs and for special counseling and tutorial services.

More often than not, Title III colleges also have critically inadequate financial resources. Small in size, they are usually unable to provide a sufficiently adequate staff or other strengths to attract and maintain a larger enrollment. Further, they often suffer from geographical isolation. They are likely to be located in areas short on cultural resources, where there is little to attract first-rate faculty, and where higher education does not have a high priority in terms of financial support. Among such colleges, a smaller proportion of faculty than usual holds appropriate degrees, and faculty salaries are characteristically lower than those in more thriving institutions. Title III colleges are apt to lack adequate administrative capabilities in organization, management, planning, budget-making, and record-keeping. Their fund-raising resources by comparison with more developed ones, are likely to be poorly organized or nonexistent (Kelly, n.d., p. 4).

Not all Title III institutions exhibit all of the characteristics described above. But one can note certain types of institutions within the group. There are public institutions which qualify as "developing" because of their geographic isolation and their service to predominantly low-income or minority groups. There are private four-year colleges which face a crisis of survival due to inadequate resources and endowment, cultural isolation, competition from growing public institutions, and an increasingly adverse differential between their tuition and that of public colleges. There are other private colleges which are in one way or another church-related and face problems because of diminishing support from church sources. There are black colleges, with long histories of inadequate support and inadequate educational strength. And there are junior and community colleges, which constitute the fastest growing element in higher education and reflect an emerging pattern of open access in educational preparation, and to which Congress directed a percentage of the Title III funds (Kelly, n.d., pp. 6–9).

These kinds of institutions display in a very acute form some needs that are endemic in higher education today: needs for general economic support, for adaptation to changing social conditions, for a clearer functional identity (particularly the church-related colleges and the black colleges); for reform in curriculum and instruction, for new student services to meet the changing needs of students, and for substantial improvement in management and organization.

The basic premise of Title III is that these kinds of institutions and their needs can be assisted substantially by institutional support which encourages and operates through cooperative arrangements with other institutions. This premise has stimulated a wide range of cooperative activities under Title III, not all of them through the kind of consortium treated in the present study. In other instances, cooperative endeavors begun with foundation support have grown through an additional input of Title III monies. For example, the College Placement Service, funded in the mid-1960s by The Ford Foundation, and now involving several dozen colleges in better career counseling and job placement for black graduates, has come to benefit indirectly from Title III support at the institutional level. But the consortia of developing institutions go far beyond the specialized or single-purpose cooperative arrangement illustrated by the College Placement Service. This pattern of applied Title III support, broadly interpreted and extensively used in the years since 1965, now appears to be reaffirmed by legislation on higher education in 1972.

New consortia throughout the United States have sprung up in response to Title III money, and older ones have turned to such funding through the ability of their institutions to justify their qualification for funding under the Act. Essentially classifiable as a service consortium within the typology suggested above, the Kansas City Regional Council for Higher Education (KCRCHE) is an example of the impact of Title III funding on existing consortia. KCRCHE antedated the Higher Education Act of 1965 by three years. It was incorporated in 1962 "to provide means for advancing higher education in the greater Kansas City area by fostering cooperative efforts on the part of member institutions" (KCRCHE, n.d.). By 1972, KCRCHE was composed of sixteen colleges and universities in eastern Kansas, western Missouri, and southern Iowa; thirteen of them private colleges and universities, and three public institutions. Its membership includes religious institutions, two-year colleges, and urban and nonurban institutions.

Although currently undergoing change at its top administrative level, KCRCHE has had a steady and active history. Supported by annual dues of four thousand dollars from each constituent member, it has been able to secure additional funding for its operations and services from a variety of sources, including private foundations, corporations, and most notably the federal government. By far the largest single part of its income in recent years has been Title III money. A Title III grant of $450,000 was awarded in 1969–70 to Rockhurst College for channeling into the activities of the consortium; in 1970—an additional $300,000 was similarly channeled; and for 1971–72 another Title III grant of $300,000 was secured. (Title III funds for such cooperative activities have been channeled in this way under the law to individual colleges, rather than to consortia directly, for routing into consortium operations.) In 1972, through Park College, KCRCHE asked for a further Title III grant for fiscal year 1973 to support essentially the same seven programs as before: (1) Academic Mutual Aid, to enable institutions to further the pooling of instructional resources and to disseminate effective instructional innovations and practices from one institution to another; (2) Faculty Development Grants; (3) Cooperative Library Resources, to extend the reader-printer services of the joint periodicals collection, to expand the joint catalogue card production service, and to further coordination of collection building and interlibrary loan procedures; (4) On-Campus Consultation, for assistance in redirecting and restructuring academic programs; (5) Student Services, to promote increased coordination of admissions, placement, and counseling services; (6) Administrative Improvement, to further the implementation of educational computer data processing and long-range planning, to expand cost-sharing activities, and to provide training opportunities for top management personnel and other administrators; and (7) Telephone Network, for support of the KCRCHE communications network (KCRCHE, 1971, p. 2).

The dependence of KCRCHE on federal support for some of its central services and activities extends well beyond Title III. In 1970, for example, the consortium contracted with Kansas City, Missouri, to provide services in connection with the Model Cities Program in the amount of $108,000, and received grants under

Title VII of the Social Security Act amounting to nearly $150,000 (KCRCHE, 1971).

Through Title III funding in the most well-staffed and vital of service consortia, like KCRCHE, groups of relatively limited and frail institutions secure a kind of leavening and stimulus which they would be unlikely to obtain in any other way. There is collective effort at improvement that seems good, even if far from the kind of joint academic planning and operation that might be ideal. In a number of other places, as in the Colleges of Mid-America (CMA)— a consortium of eleven small church-related institutions in Iowa and South Dakota—Title III funding has some of the same results but seems on balance simply a convenient way of pumping federal funds into small institutions.

In both CMA and KCRCHE, the number of institutions involved and the geographical distances separating them militate against very close cooperative academic planning and development. Not much long-range planning of any kind is visible either in CMA or KCRCHE. But in the Colleges of Mid-America planning is something that the presidents at least mention as an aspiration, and in KCRCHE planning for academic cooperation is being seriously talked about by the academic deans. In 1971, the KCRCHE academic deans called for more regional coordination and for giving priority to cooperative educational efforts among the KCRCHE institutions in seven areas: exchange of faculty, exchange of students, complementary instructional curricula, shared faculty, shared consultants, pooled data for institutional research, and institutes and group meetings of faculty. Such recommendations could be an augury of closer academic cooperation in this consortium.

In summary, one is struck by the diversity and complexity, and by the uneven development, of the groups of institutions in this study. Only a very few, principally those that I have labeled as cooperative consortia, appear to be entering into anything like close joint educational planning and operation. Even in the best of these, institutional autonomy and self-interest remains the predominant pattern, and cooperative endeavors appear thin. For the most part, these cooperative consortia have small institutional memberships that occupy relatively small geographical areas.

The greatest number of consortia in the present study are what I call service-oriented. They engage in relatively little close academic cooperation; they are likely to have ten to twenty member institutions, separated sometimes by great distances; and they commonly have a central office with a "strong" identity, operating almost as a separate agency. Increasingly, these consortia, and even some that feature academic cooperation of a closer kind, are dependent on federal funding.

At this writing, it is unclear what the typology of the consortium movement will become in the next five to ten years. Given the legislation of 1972 and the habituated dependence of a number of institutions on support like Title III to keep an educational spark going, it seems highly unlikely that the consortium movement will dissolve. But it is uncertain what directions will emerge as characteristic features of the movement. One possibility is that the service consortia, like Colleges of Mid-America, will simply continue, acting as conduits for federal funding and providing some uplift. Another possibility is that illustrated by the College Center of the Finger Lakes, where a cutting back and reorganization seems to have been a healthy thing in terms of strengthening the remaining institutions through effective academic planning and cooperation. Thus within some of the larger aggregations that appeared in the 1960s, sorting out and reorganization may occur, enabling smaller groups of institutions with kindred needs and possibilities to enter into closer, more productive cooperative association.

Chapter 3

GETTING AND SPENDING: THE ECONOMICS OF CONSORTIA

Laymen strange to the Looking-Glass economics of higher education are likely to find consortia disappointing, just as they are
sometimes appalled when they perceive the realities of finances in a
single institution. Business people, accustomed to notions of cost-
benefit analysis, budget control, rationalization of production and
division of labor, productivity measurement, and the like, are apt to
be puzzled and frequently irritated by the relative absence of these
notions in a good part of higher education. The prime rationale for
interinstitutional cooperation, it often seems to them, should be to
enable individual institutions to benefit economically by associating
with others and, by joint management of relatively scarce resources,
to allocate these resources to educational needs more efficiently.

The rhetoric of the consortium movement also suggests that cooperation should be pursued because of its possible economic benefits. In the fall of 1971 a major reorganization of the State University of New York system was designed in part to realize economies through "cooperation with private colleges and universities" and through "sharing of resources among State University units within a region" (New York *Times,* 1971, p. 1). At the same time, in discussing a proposed cooperative venture between Boston University and the University of Massachusetts, presidents John Silber and Robert Wood stated that it is "imperative for institutions to work together in developing resources, in avoiding duplication of efforts, in maintaining and improving quality" (*The Boston Globe,* 1971, p. 31). Economist David W. Breneman, who has specialized in the economics of education, comments that "cooperative programs offer potentially large savings by economizing in the use of expensive resources such as facilities and faculty" (1971, p. 3).

With such a rationale in mind, it must be especially hard to understand statements like that of Lewis Patterson: "One of the few clear-cut answers regarding financial implications of consortia is that an institution will increase its operational costs, not diminish them, as a result of joining a multipurpose consortium (1971b, p. 20).

On entering a consortium, an institution usually increases its costs in terms of assessments and dues and, less directly, by what can amount to a very substantial expenditure of time by its administrative and faculty personnel. The institution usually will receive in return, even in the case of the weaker consortia, some enrichment of its educational program, one way or another. A question very often raised by institutional leadership is whether this enrichment is worth the additional cost.

It is at the heart of the problem of the consortium that almost nowhere is the economic question asked at a deeper level than this. The innocent layman's question is more basic: How can interinstitutional cooperation enable more efficient allocation of limited resources to virtually unlimited needs? This form of the question is not being seriously asked by the institutional leadership of the consortium movement as yet. That it is not testifies less to a failure of imagination on the part of consortium leadership than to the survival of institutional autonomy as an obstacle to cooperation of anything more than a relatively nominal kind.

Aside from the fact that hopeful expectations of economy are not notably being realized, the economics of consortia present a virtually unexplored field. According to Breneman: "Although one can foresee a growing interest in cooperative programs, very little is actually known about the costs and benefits of such activities. In part this is due to conceptual problems that make it difficult to identify and measure educational and interinstitutional program costs and benefits; however, much of our ignorance simply reflects the lack of prior research on the topic. As an academic discipline, the economics of education is still in its infancy, and most of the research in this area undertaken by economists during the last ten years has not been focused upon the *institutions* of higher education. Consequently, although a topic of considerable theoretical and practical importance, the economics of interinstitutional cooperation remains poorly understood and in need of research" (1971, p. 4).

The following pages do not pretend to add much to the research literature on the economics of interinstitutional cooperation; instead they examine some empirical economic data and note their possible implications for future institutional and government policy.

The Economics of Cooperative Consortia

While adequate economic studies do not yet exist, it may be instructive to look at the economy of an academic consortium which is operating without Title III funding. Five Colleges, Incorporated, already introduced in Chapter Two, provides an interesting case in point.

Currently, each of the Five College institutions is facing some of the financial stresses that are familiar throughout higher education. Three of the four private colleges—Amherst, Mount Holyoke, and Smith—are extraordinarily well endowed in comparison with most other private institutions; but Hampshire College has virtually no endowment and, to survive, must soon come to a point where its operations are paid for by regular income. The University of Massachusetts at Amherst, by far the largest campus of the state system, has enjoyed relatively generous public funding for operations and capital outlay in most of the past twelve years, but it is now facing constraints which reflect the fact that the Massachusetts state budget is pressing against the limits of existing state tax resources.

As of the end of fiscal year 1971, Amherst, Mount Holyoke, and Smith Colleges were showing negative operating results which totaled one and a half million dollars. A study at that time projected that the negative operating results would increase over the next five years to something over four million dollars per annum. The major part of this negative position could be accounted for by an imbalance between income and expenses related chiefly to instruction. These three private institutions were in a position to cover their negative operating results out of available capital resources and reserves for the foreseeable future, but the demand on capital resources and reserves would be increased. The chief strategy of each institution, faced with this reality, was to seek increasing private support beyond usual income to sustain their operations. An alternative or supplementary strategy, given the existence of Five College cooperation, would have been to try more actively to secure financial benefits from academic cooperation.

The situation of Hampshire College at the end of fiscal year 1971 was different from that of its three private sisters only because its financial problems were more severe and immediate. Its trustees and administration had recognized the dynamics of this situation from the beginning of planning the college, and had developed tight internal budgetary guidelines to make the institution's financial management efficient. In pursuit of the goal of balancing income and operating expenses, they established a sixteen-to-one student-faculty ratio; limited appointments in faculty rank to a one-two-four ratio of professors, associate professors, and assistant professors; and adopted a system of faculty appointments on limited contract, excluding the possibility of life tenure. Thus Hampshire sought to limit ongoing instructional costs from within, while at the same time relying on Five College academic cooperation to permit it to economize in its curricular offerings.

As a public institution, the University of Massachusetts at Amherst was in a different position from that of the private colleges in the Five College consortium. Over the 1960s it had expanded rapidly at the undergraduate and graduate levels, adding significantly both to the numbers and quality of its faculty. At the beginning of the 1970s it continued to secure operating income support relatively easily while at the same time controlling its instructional costs by a standard fifteen-to-one student-faculty ratio and careful internal and external financial oversight. But this situation began to change as the 1970s opened because of two factors: the creation of two new University campuses at Boston and Worcester, and the growing tendency of the Commonwealth to restrict educational expenditures as a function of the general fiscal stringency faced by state government.

Given this financial condition of the five institutions involved, one might expect great momentum toward academic cooperation within Five Colleges, Incorporated. It might be thought, for example, that there would have developed a very substantial reliance on student interchange and faculty interchange in pursuit of institutional economies in instruction. But while the past four years have shown a dramatic increase in student interchange, such activity still represents no more than 3 percent of all course enrollments in the consortium. Perhaps more important, such interchange appears to be primarily student-initiated instead of the result of interinstitutional planning. Students simply take advantage of the general openness to interchange enrollment on a relatively random basis, rather than enrolling under a planned system of educational complementarity designed to use institutional and instructional resources more efficiently. One clear motivation for student-initiated interchange is to have the experience of coeducation, since Amherst, Mount Holyoke, and Smith students presently account for a significant number of interchange enrollments.

Faculty interchange similarly is small in size and similarly is generally unplanned, usually arising to cover unexpected or emergency requirements at another institution on a moonlighting basis, instead of being worked out as part of planned academic complementarity.

Thus while it is true that Five Colleges, Incorporated is one of the most developed cooperative consortia in the country, it is also true that its economy does not yet reflect a significant, planned effort to address the financial realities of academic operations among its constituent institutions. Since the spring of 1971, it has moved some distance in coordinating course offerings to enhance the economic utility of student and faculty interchange, but there is still a long way to go. The difficulties involved, and the need for better inter-institutional economic and financial planning, are made clear by Breneman (1971, p. 5) :

> A major component of the cooperative program is student-course exchange, a program which allows a student from any of the five colleges to take a course for credit at a neighboring institution at no direct expense to the student. The course exchange has grown rapidly, from a total of 581 semester exchanges in 1966–67 to 2352 in 1970–71. When first begun, the private colleges established a fee system, with the institution from which a student comes paying the receiving institution one hundred fifty dollars per semester course (because of state regulations, the University is not involved in this system of money payments). The fee was originally set in relation to the tuition charges at the colleges, and was not based upon analysis of the cost of instruction. Recently, one of the colleges experienced a "balance of payments" problem for it was "exporting" many more of its own students to the other four schools than it was "importing" students from those schools. Faced with having to make sizeable payments to the other institutions, the deficit college responded in precisely the manner that a student of international trade would predict—it imposed barriers to the free flow of students. Rather than allow the system of course exchanges to contract, or possibly collapse, the colleges agreed to suspend the fee payment for a two-year period, during which time the matter would be reconsidered. This problem, currently confronting the Five College program, is amenable to economic analysis; ideally, one would want a system of fees that reflects the marginal cost to the host institution of adding a student from another school to a particular class. In many cases the marginal cost may effectively be zero (e.g., one student added to a lecture class of fifty) ; in other cases, the presence of students from another school may properly be viewed as imposing a cost on the host institution, and a positive fee might be in order. Economic analysis, both conceptual and empirical, will be necessary if a rational fee structure is to be established that accurately reflects the costs involved,

The economic analysis that Breneman indicates as needed would be an instrumental part of more practical planning for academic complementarity. Needed in addition are many other things, including careful ongoing identification of (1) low-demand disciplines in terms of course enrollments and majors per faculty, (2) course offerings with substantial overlap, and (3) specific ways in which reductions in total academic resources could be made without damaging the overall quality of programs. It remains to be seen whether these kinds of steps will be adequately taken by Five Colleges, Incorporated.

The Economics of Service and Title III Consortia

Aside from institutional membership fees and special charges for services rendered, the central fact in the economics of service and Title III consortia is external funding. The major proportion by far of such external funding is from federal sources; the dimensions of which are suggested by the fact that Title III expenditures in fiscal 1972 amounted to over fifty-one million dollars, with authorization in fiscal 1973 sought at the level of one hundred million dollars.

But beyond Title III, federal funds come to consortia under other legislation: Title II–C of the Higher Education Act of 1965 has provided special-purpose grants aimed at bringing together library systems through cooperative means. The United States Office of Education also has funded a Consortium Research Development Program (CORD) to stimulate educational research by faculty members in small universities and colleges. The National Science Foundation has entered the field to support cooperative programs in science education and scientific research. One of its better known offices, the College Science Improvement Program (COSIP), has funded cooperative improvements in undergraduate science education as well as single-institution improvement. And other federal agencies and programs not directly related to education, such as the Model Cities Program and the Social Security Administration, sometimes fund consortia projects, as in the case of KCRCHE.

External funding has also come from private foundations, but the pace of support has slowed notably in the past several years. The Danforth Foundation, for example, continues to maintain an interest in the consortium movement, but in an individual comment as early as 1968, one of its vice-presidents suggested a future pattern of foundation relationship to consortia: "The honeymoon, if there ever was one, is over. The development of consortia has proved a success. Established consortia will find foundation funding increasingly difficult to obtain for more of the same type of programs or for their continuation. In turn, newly established consortia will have difficulty in attracting foundation funds for efforts which would duplicate programs already in existence in other consortia" (Zimmerman, 1968, p. 7).

Part of the reluctance of foundations to continue helping consortia stems from an understandable disinclination to support on-going services which should presumably be part of the expected budgeting of constituent institutions. Part of it comes as well from the knowledge that Title III and other federal funding has been increasingly available to subsidize consortia services and operations. And part it must be admitted, comes from a well-funded skepticism about claims that consortium cooperation is leading toward planned academic complementarity and the rationalization of economic operations in higher education.

Under Title III support, as in so many other cases of federal aid to education, a kind of improvisational patchworking does less than it should to insure the upgrading of central consortium operations, promote coherent long-range planning, or provide incentives for planned academic complementarity. As noted in Chapter Two, Title III grants are made directly to institutions rather than to consortia, even though participation in a cooperative arrangement is a condition for the grants. Their intent has been institutional improvement, allowing each institution to determine the extent to which it will participate in cooperative arrangements. This stance has discouraged whatever impulses toward coherent consortium planning might exist: Lack of direct fiscal control places the Title III consortium at a disadvantage when it comes to the implementation of agreed-upon plans; while channeling funds through institutions to the consortium involves unnecessary negotiation and the possibility that some funds may never be fully available for the purpose intended. Some Title III consortia have handled this difficulty better than others, but, as Father Kelly pointed out, the

Title III pattern as a whole has tended to put central consortium offices at both an economic and policy disadvantage (n.d., pp. 46–47).

The Hazards of Specificity

In terms of long-run planning and development, the external funding of consortia has not tended to further the cause of cooperation as much as it could have done. External funding, whether from federal or foundation sources, has been characterized by a peculiar, short-sighted specificity. Federal monies are generally for very specific programs—a shared clinical psychologist, for example, or the development of a cross–catalog of library holdings. There are virtually no monies available, either from federal or foundation sources, for planning. Foundations, too, support specific consortium projects that are likely to be locked into a short-term operational specificity and do not contribute to long-term planned development.

At this stage in the history of consortia, it is important that the federal government and the foundations recognize the need for long-range consortium planning. Consortia have a critical lack of planning funds, not geared to the production of specific projects, but aimed toward evaluating present progress, analyzing specific institutional economic positions as they are relevant to the potentialities of cooperation, determining reasonable goals for consortium development, and devising ways and means to maximize complementarity and possible educational and economic benefits that may accrue through cooperation.

This need would seem to be more appropriate for consideration by foundations than by the federal government. It appears likely that federal support for consortium operations under Title III may continue, and it is clear that foundations cannot support consortium operating expenses in any wholesale fashion. But foundations could do a great deal to improve the quality of the movement by selective grants to stimulate consortia planning and more intelligent use of increasingly available federal funds.

Two instances illustrate the utility of strong long-range planning by consortia. One is the case of Five Colleges, Incorporated, where partial use of a hundred-thousand-dollar grant from the

Richard King Mellon Foundation not only helped the consortium to produce its highly regarded planning report, but also explicitly enabled it to try new academic programs. While Five Colleges, Incorporated still has a long way to go in achieving high-order academic cooperation, this grant made a significant difference in the history of that consortium. In the case of the College Center of the Finger Lakes, CCFL produced an excellent planning document, *Patterns for Voluntary Cooperation,* in 1971 in spite of the absence of special funding. Help by a foundation would have been entirely appropriate in this case.

Most of the consortia visited in the course of this study have revealed a serious need for this kind of planning. Consortium directors have declared wistfully their desire to do something comparable, but they have been constrained by the day-to-day demands of business as usual and have had neither the money nor the personnel to undertake substantial self-study or planning. It would be advantageous for every consortium to undertake an in-depth self-study at least every five years. Almost none has done this, with the result that the consortia are benefited neither by adequate self-scrutiny nor by orderly and imaginative planning for the future.

Danger from the IRS

That the economic life of the consortium is not necessarily either simple or happy, is attested to by current embroilment of consortia with the Internal Revenue Service. For reasons that are not altogether clear, the IRS is threatening seriously the cooperative activities of colleges and universities by putting the tax exempt status of consortia in jeopardy. The consortium movement, therefore, is in the peculiar position of being encouraged by the federal government through legislation like that in Title III while simultaneously being shot down by the IRS. With a friend like the federal government, who needs an enemy?

The IRS position makes it appear that an organization controlled by and operated for the benefit of a group of tax exempt institutions, performing a function which each institution would otherwise have to perform for itself, will not be recognized as exempt unless it provides the service to its member institutions for a charge "substantially below cost." Furthermore, the Service has indicated that such a cooperative activity will lose its exemption if more than 15 percent of the costs are borne by the member institutions, each of which is itself exempt.

The thinking behind this position appears to be based upon Section 502 of the Internal Revenue Code of 1954. When Congress imposed a tax on the unrelated trade or business of exempt organizations, it included this section to make sure that exempt organizations would not attempt to avoid the tax by means of an incorporated subsidiary. Strict interpretation by the IRS of this section has been of continuing difficulty to groups of hospitals and is now affecting groups of colleges and universities. As John Holt Myers has put it:

> The thrust of the Service's ruling policies is that a cooperative venture of colleges and universities . . . cannot be exempt unless it is, in effect, totally supported from sources outside the member institutions. This simply is not possible in the case of the usual college and university consortium. Traditionally, such an organization may find outside support for the start-up costs involved in the organization and initial operation of such an activity. Invariably, there is no reason to expect that any such cooperative venture, however important to education, would be endowed or that a continuation of grants for its support may be expected. Member institutions themselves obviously must expect to assume a major portion of the expenses of an activity appropriate to the carrying on of its exempt functions which is carried on through the joint venture. . . .
>
> It would appear . . . that the Internal Revenue Service presently intends to adhere to its position with respect to the regulations under Section 502. . . . Thus, unless statutory relief is obtained, the Internal Revenue Service position will specifically threaten those numerous joint activities of educational institutions, even those which are being forced upon colleges and universities by federal and state granting agencies. It is significant to note also that if the Internal Revenue Service position is allowed to persist, the result will be to force the termination of many existing cooperative activities, and that there is no real possibility of any tax revenue being produced. The real burden of such action will fall on the small institutions whose future may well depend on cooperative action to improve

quality and save expense. Under the circumstances, it would appear that legislative relief is the only practical recourse [Myers, 1972].

Legislative relief has not yet been secured, although it may be possible to obtain such relief from Congress in 1974. In view of the facts, it is difficult to imagine that Congress will deny consortia exemption from taxation, but the situation currently is not an easy one. If the economics of the consortium movement is to conform to the expectations of Congress, it certainly will be necessary for it to have a more favorable tax context than presently exists.

In short, if the public interest and the interest of institutions are both to be served, the economics of cooperation need continuous study and appropriate action both by consortia themselves and by other agencies in which relevant policy is made. There is a considerable need, as Breneman points out, for professional economists to turn their attention to this aspect of higher education. There is an even greater need for consortia themselves to understand the economic realities and potentialities of cooperation as these relate to the survival and quality of individual institutions. It is impossible to divorce economics from essential considerations of interinstitutional cooperation, unless one is prepared to settle, as many consortia appear to be willing to do, for the shadow of cooperation rather than its substance. Economic studies of and by consortia should be part of the general forward planning that the movement so drastically lacks at this stage.

A major obstacle to genuine confrontation of the economic aspects of interinstitutional cooperation is the tenaciousness of institutional autonomy behind the facade of cooperation. Title III and other federal support is doing little to remove this obstacle because support tends to subsidize discrete projects and programs which have little impact on such things as substantial planned complementarity among institutions.

It is important for foundations to understand this situation, and instead of being put off by the shallowness of much of the movement, to provide incentive funding which will stimulate a higher level of cooperative development than now exists. It is specifically this situation which contains promise but lacks performance that selective foundation grants, requiring tough-minded self-examination and long-range planning, could change for the better.

The further need, for a coherent favorable federal attitude of support, is underlined by the present contradiction between IRS rulings and Congressional legislation like that in Title III. By providing more financial incentives and removing the threat of IRS intervention, Congress could materially push otherwise autonomy-oriented institutions into more genuinely efficient economic use of the consortium mechanism. Institutions will not achieve significant new levels of economic advantage through consortia without such external incentive or pressure.

Chapter 4

GOVERNANCE AND DECISION-MAKING

Aside from the impact of federal funding, the economics of consortia take their current configuration in response to two principal factors. One is the continuing tendency of participating institutions to pursue essentially autonomous directions no matter what consortium umbrella they gather under. The second, closely related, is the predominant tendency of consortium members to leave governance in the hands of institutional presidents, who themselves represent institutional autonomy and who reflect the competing constituency pressures and decision-making processes internal to their institutions. Both factors help account for the very limited power of consortium executive directors. And both account for the fact that most consortia, as yet, are more facade and rhetoric than substance.

In their essence, the majority of formal consortium arrangements feature a simple form of governance: a board of directors consisting of the presidents of the member institutions, which sets

43

policy and oversees the implementing actions of the executive director and his staff. The consortium board is likely to meet regularly. A few boards have monthly meetings, a few have annual meetings; the largest number meet on a quarterly or semiannual basis. Board chairmanship is usually carried by one of the presidents, elected by his fellows. Meeting attendance usually is good, and in typical board fashion, the members address themselves to a set agenda, which the executive director has helped prepare, supported by committee and staff documents. When the institutional membership of a consortium is large or geographically diffuse or both, ongoing board actions between regular meetings are usually handled by an executive committee.

Beneath the board of directors one finds a number of interinstitutional committees, characteristically with one member from each institution and served by the executive director and his staff. Executive directors find these committees valuable especially for the exchange of fresh and useful ideas across institutional lines, the development of faculty commitment to the consortium, and the development of new programs for board consideration. The multiplicity of such committees in some consortia is astonishing. Piedmont University Center features ten standing committees with a total membership of 209, while Associated Colleges of the Midwest has had thirty-one standing committees with a total membership of 274 (Piedmont University Center, 1972, pp. 12–21; ACM, 1970; *Papers*, 1972, pp. 34–68). The sheer number and activities of committees heavily occupy the time and energy of executive directors and their staffs.

Where committee and staff work are genuinely productive, they bring to the board reasonably adequate background for making decisions. The degree of consortium maturity and presidential commitment to interinstitutional cooperation tend to affect whether such materials are adequate and whether they have full attention and consideration by the board. It seems fair to say that in more than a few consortia, interinstitutional committee work is more nominal than substantial, while it is not infrequent that thorough committee studies receive only nominal attention at board level. Both conditions are part of the symptomology of weakness that char-

acterizes interinstitutional consortia generally in terms of fundamental academic complementarity and economic cooperation.

Governance in Service Consortia

While it is difficult to generalize about all consortia, service
consortia have certain characteristics of governance which appear
to be specific to the category. They tend to be large in terms of the
number of member institutions and geographical area covered,
which is likely to mean that the governing board—made up of constituent institutional presidents—is also relatively large and unable
to meet conveniently with any great frequency. As a decision-making body the service consortium board is less than likely to involve
president–directors deeply or frequently, and one gains the impression that a seat on the board of a service consortium tends to rate
very low in a college president's priorities. There is no instance, for
example, where any member institution's financial commitment to
a service consortium has exceeded one-half of one percent of that
institution's operating budget; and only very rarely does an institution's out-of-pocket membership commitment approach the cost of
a single faculty member's salary. If the out-of-pocket costs were
higher, one might expect consortium affairs to have a greater claim
on the attention of president-directors.

Characteristically, the presidents of participating institutions
have little connection with the programatic operations of the typical
service consortium, such as the year abroad, library services, or off-
campus science semesters. These are supplements to his institution's
essential program, are usually paid for by fees or special project
funding, and are managed by staff, frequently with the active involvement of special or detached faculty. As long as such programs
do not get into trouble (with trouble usually construed as financial
demands made directly on participating institutions), the president-
directors are not likely to give them more than passing attention.

Size and possible expansion seem to be natural to the structure and operation of the service consortium. Central operations, as
well as supplementary programs, self-evidently cost each institution
less if expenditures can be spread over more institutions. Raising the

dues and fees is invariably unpopular and problematic; it is simpler to attract more members, thereby gaining more dues and fees, more potential customers for special programs, and presumably more comprehensive wisdom at the board level of policy planning and decision making.

But being elephantine has its disadvantages, too. Any new program or change in emphasis must ultimately be considered by a board which may number twenty or more and which may not meet as a body for months at a time. The need to achieve consensus on such a program tends to guarantee its blandness and causes difficulty in terminating a failing program since anyone defending the program tends to be sustained out of a kind of "senatorial courtesy." The larger the governing body the more remote is the possibility of securing agreement to raise dues or fees. And in addition, the executive director becomes both more and less powerful. He is more powerful since he is the only member of the governing structure who knows what is happening; but he is weaker for the same reason. The board of a consortium, made up of presidents, is more than a little like a group of barons. The greater their number and the less their interinstitutional affinity, the more likely the executive director is to be able to keep his hand on the helm of daily operations. But woe betide him if the operations offend his barons or endanger what any one of them sees as the self-interest of his own domain.

The executive director can lead, under existing consortium patterns, only through persuasion. The larger the board of directors the more various and consuming are the requirements of persuasion that he must meet. Fear of failing to provide that which the board expects, with the board standing somewhat distantly from actual operations, tends to rigidify the executive director's approach to the consortium program. The central direction becomes devoted to maintenance at the expense of innovation.

One consortium I visited suggests how hard the arteries can become under these conditions. The executive director put it succinctly when he stated that his presidents were happy, and that he, therefore, saw no new directions needed for the consortium. On the other hand, fiscal constraints are so severe that he cannot provide the services he provided five years ago through central staff operations, and yet he does not dare raise fees for fear of losing members. Indeed, one of the member institutions is considering dropping out of the consortium because of a sense that returns from it are diminishing. Thus the consortium is simply sitting tight, unable to maintain or improve existing operations, let alone add new services.

Out of all this, it is not unreasonable to conclude that the governance of the service consortium is customarily organized in ways inappropriate to the best performance of its ascribed functions. In a genuine sense, the function of a service consortium is analogous to that of a mercantile establishment. It has services to sell and seeks buyers. If one buys a car a year, one does not expect to be on the board of the dealership. Yet many universities and colleges are paying far less than the annual cost of an automobile for service consortium dues, and their presidents sit on the governing board. The actual dollar volume of such consortia operations is far larger than the institutional investment in membership fees: The operating expenses are not paid by dues; instead they are usually derived from program participant fees and special project funds secured from federal and foundation sources.

To pursue the analogy of the mercantile establishment further, the president-directors are nonconsumers, or consumers only in a limited and very detached way. Put another way, they are not directly enough concerned with securing the benefits of the consortium or maintaining and developing its quality to be its appropriate governors. Save for a tradition that the heads of institutions ought to be at the top, I see no reason why the board of presidents model of governance for service consortia should exist. The providing of services to institutions of education can more appropriately be organized, governed, and managed by persons external to these institutions. Examples of efficiency and success in this connection exist in the food service organizations which have grown up in the past quarter century, none of whose boards of directors is composed of the presidents of the institutions it feeds. Instead, institutions contract with these independent organizations for services if they so desire, retaining their own institutional autonomy, but benefiting by services rendered through a specialized organization with larger resources and capabilities than any single institution can muster.

It can reasonably be argued that educational service consortia should be governed by those who have the most direct stake in rendering both high quality and economically attractive services. The first perceived objective of institutional presidents is to save money—to maintain a minimal investment in consortium operations with the hope that something good will happen. It is quite possible to imagine a radical alternative in which the educational service organization would exist independently of institutions served, would be either a nonprofit or a profit-making corporation, and would be governed by persons with a direct commitment to its success in serving colleges and universities economically and with high educational quality. Such a board with a direct commitment, including cash investments, would probably show more imagination and interest than would the busy heads of twenty or so institutions, meeting at long intervals and committed only to minimal annual dues. Its fortunes would rise or fall in terms of quality, attractiveness, and financial feasibility of the services it offered to institutions.

Aside from having a governing body directly committed to the success of the organization, this alternative model could in many ways resemble the better-staffed existing service consortia. Effectively, the institutional customers of the service organization would constitute a collective as much as do the members of most service consortia today. But governance would rest with those with a thorough knowledge of its services and a strong financial interest in its success. Governance would be highly centralized not diffuse. And a strong executive would be in charge, rather than preoccupied with keeping his band of institutional barons happy.

Governance in Cooperative Consortia

The cooperative consortium presents a different set of conditions for governance. Cooperation requires that the chief executive officers of the participating colleges and universities sit on the governing board of the consortium. Only the presidents can commit their institutions to significant academic cooperation or to other major cooperative arrangements. Their direct guidance and commitment of support are essential. To the degree they play a genuine leadership role, the cooperative consortium may move toward planned complementarity and productive collaboration.

While ultimate decision-making power in a cooperative consortium must therefore be vested in the presidents, a consortium of this kind can diffuse subordinate operating leadership among the participating institutions in order to secure continuing initiative on each campus and maintain an active interplay among the institutions through consortium-related officers responsible both to their individual institutions and to the consortium. In this connection, the College Center of the Finger Lakes is experimenting with a very promising form of governance: Its executive director is located in a consortium headquarters wholly unconnected with any participating institution—an arrangement often found in other consortia—but an assistant director is located at each member campus.

Each assistant director, a senior faculty member who serves half-time as CCFL representative, is chosen by the president of each institution with an eye toward the following qualifications: (1) good personal relationship with the president and the consortium executive director; (2) commitment to the concept of interinstitutional cooperation in general and to CCFL in particular; (3) ambassadorial ability; (4) good standing with the faculty at his home institution; and (5) interest in a particular aspect of CCFL operations. The principal mission of the assistant director in the new CCFL organization is to work towards making the consortium as integral a part of his own campus as is the institution's own autonomous program. He is responsible for managing a separate aspect of the entire consortium, as well as being the chief campus representative for all consortium activities. The executive director of CCFL hopes that these positions will become full-time as the new system develops.

Although such decentralization of consortium leadership and management may be more important for an association like CCFL, where individual institutions are separated from each other by significant distances, than it would be for cooperative ventures where the distance is minimal, nonetheless it would seem that an on-campus consortium presence at each institution would be a decided asset for any genuine cooperative effort. The advantages of having a well-qualified academic, identified both as a member of the home team and as the consortium representative by the administration, faculty, and student body are substantial. Such a representative can maintain continuity of communication, allay fears, suggest advantages, provide initiative, accomplish necessary groundwork, and in essence play a dual role of faculty anchorman and consortium evangelist from a position of trust. Thus the Five College Long-Range Planning Committee has recommended that "each institution should establish the position of Five College Deputy, make clear his focal role in cooperation, and appoint to the position a senior faculty or academic staff member, to be released from a major portion of his other duties, for a term of at least three years" (1969, pp. 181–182).

Another way to diffuse responsibility for policy development and operating management among participating institutions is illustrated by The Association for Graduate Education and Research of North Texas (TAGER), which is governed jointly by a Board of Trustees and a Board of Governing Participants. Its Board of Trustees holds the legal authority of the consortium and is responsible for determining matters of policy and for managing TAGER's physical assets. This board is composed of two representatives from each of the four participating institutions (Southern Methodist University, Texas Christian University, University of Dallas, and the University of Texas at Dallas), three representatives elected from the community at large by the preceding eight, and the chairman of the Board of Governing Participants *ex officio*—currently James M. Moudy, Chancellor of Texas Christian University.

In turn, the Board of Governing Participants is composed of the chief executive officer of each participant and associate participant institution, and senior representative of an industrial firm served by TAGER, and one faculty representative from a TAGER institution. This board supervises academic programs, oversees the operating management of the consortium, and in general sets the agenda for the Board of Trustees. Serving the Board of Governing Participants is the Academic Planning Committee, composed of the chief academic officer of each participating institution. Thus TAGER builds into its top governance a considerable diffusion of responsibility for planning and decision-making among leaders of institutions in the group.

At the level of operating management, Chancellor Moudy has established a half-time Deputy for TAGER Affairs at the TCU campus and is hopeful that a similar post will be created on each of the other campuses. The system would then be somewhat like that of CCFL, with a deputy on each campus providing follow-through on Academic Planning Committee decisions. With only three persons on TAGER's central staff to operate its interinstitutional programs among eight institutions of higher education and eleven corporations, this system would assure consortium presence at the institutional level.

In some ways, the most complex governing structure of a cooperative consortium belongs to The Claremont Colleges. Since it initiated cooperative interinstitutional development in 1925, this group has written and rewritten many constitutions—in 1941, 1950, 1951, 1962, and 1967—prior to the latest revision in 1970. Its resulting structure is extraordinarily complex, featuring seven different boards, committees, and councils. The Claremont Colleges are geared toward accomplishing five objectives: (1) to develop a center of undergraduate and graduate learning, yet (2) provide the personal instruction and other educational advantages inherent in the small college, together with (3) the facilities, advantages, resources, and intellectual climate found in universities of the highest quality; (4) permit interchange of students and faculty; and (5) maintain colleges of limited enrollment and found new member colleges when practicable (Council of the Claremont Colleges, 1970).

To accomplish these ends, the five undergraduate colleges and graduate school are overseen by their individual boards of trustees, with restraints imposed on them by the charter of The Claremont University Center, which is governed by several boards of which two are preeminent: The Executive Committee of the Board of Fellows, and The Council of The Claremont Colleges. The Executive Committee of the Board of Fellows, which is composed of the several presidents and the chairmen of their respective boards of trustees and is responsible for nominating the president of the Graduate School and nominating the chancellor, appointing the provost, and nominating key financial personnel, such as the treasurer, essentially performs a ratifying rather than policy-setting function. The Council of The Claremont Colleges, composed of the several presidents and the chancellor, is responsible for setting policy for the chancellor and the provost. Thus, when we unravel what appeared to be an extraordinarily complicated and diffuse governmental structure, we find our old friend, governance by a board of presidents.

Under the three chief bodies—the Executive Committee of the Board of Fellows, the Board of Fellows itself, and the Council of The Claremont Colleges—the consortium operates through four ancillary organizations. One of these is the Standing Committee of Future Colleges, whose title rather clearly defines its function. Its membership? The several presidents, the chairmen of their respective boards of trustees, and the chancellor. The other three are the Claremont Colleges Board of Overseers, the Intercollegiate Council, and the Joint Committee on Ways and Means. These bodies appear to be designed to serve two purposes: to provide additional breadth of participation in policy review and development and to broaden the fund-raising base for the Claremont group. The presidents sit on all but the Board of Overseers, and the board chairmen of the participating institutions sit on all three of these governance bodies.

Role of Trustees. Aside from its complexity, a feature of Claremont Colleges governance which sets it apart from other cooperative efforts is the relatively deep involvement of the chairmen of the boards of trustees of the participating institutions. The long stability and steady development of the Claremont group probably results in good part from this involvement, which adds substantially to the interaction and leadership provided by the group of presidents. No other consortium approaches Claremont in the degree of trustee involvement; one would expect that consortia interested in maximizing cooperation would seek to learn from the Claremont experience.

Trustee involvement at Greensboro Tri-College Consortium has also provided a significant impetus toward cooperative efforts. Through the leadership of the late board chairman of Guilford College, the Board of Trustees of Guilford set up a rigid set of policy guidelines which has functioned to encourage cooperation by requiring that Guilford as a whole and all its divisions and departments individually must operate without a deficit. This has meant, for example, that if a specific department is lagging in enrollments relative to its faculty costs, it has three basic options: to promote itself among Guilford students (perhaps at the expense of other departments); to close; or to combine efforts with another institution. The first two options, interestingly enough, have not proved as attractive to Guilford departments as has the third, with the result that Guilford participation in the Greensboro Tri-College Consortium has grown: its president has been able to direct departments in trouble toward cooperation in a way that would have been difficult without trustee interest in the benefits of interinstitutional collaboration.

I have suggested that the presidential board does not necessarily best serve the interests of service consortia, in that governance by presidents alone results in relatively weak service. I feel that trustee involvement in service consortia would be equally counterproductive for the same basic reasons. But the different conditions which affect cooperative consortia and Title III consortia argue for strong trustee involvement. Where a president does not have the luxury of time to concentrate on the consortium, a trustee may. Trustees enmeshed in the planning and operations of a consortium can serve an invaluable role in representing its interests to institutional boards and institutional presidents. By establishing such participation, cooperative consortia would be better equipped to survive one of their most consistent pitfalls—the departure of a strong, interested president from a key member institution.

Trustee involvement can also help establish the consortium in the local community, offer sound business since it removes the "one-man-in-the middle" problem faced by many presidents, and be very useful in determining the consortium's role because trustees are often able to develop a detached perspective nearly impossible for a president or an executive director, concentrated as they are in day-to-day operations. But the most important reason for trustee involvement is the nature of their mission. They are the policy-setters for their institutions. Their long-term interests are the membership's long-term interest, which in turn, are the consortium's long-term interest. The ultimate power to set policy has not been present in the governance of most consortia, resulting in the absence of decisive direction. Therefore consortia must begin to develop stronger ties with the governing bodies of their membership institutions.

Role of Faculty. By and large, consortia are products of academic administration. They are founded by presidents, operated by administrators, and serve member institutions by providing expanded administrative and service resources such as computing networks and joint purchasing. Even the disciplinary resources they provide are, more often than not, geared towards students rather than faculty. There is much concern in the field over this issue. All executive directors I interviewed felt faculty-consortium interaction to be both highly desirable and very low.

The service consortium is constrained by definition. It lacks the physical presence necessary for faculty involvement. Faculty traditionally serve two roles for such consortia: as their institution's representative on program steering committees and as the on-campus contact for the particular programs the school has entered. The benefits to the involved faculty member are minor: a chance to attend a number of meetings and perhaps a chance for some foreign travel. There is little that a service consortium can offer a faculty member that gives direct benefit to his standing within his department and within his discipline. The faculty member's connection with a service consortium is strictly administrative and will remain so as long as the consortium is so constituted.

In theory, the Title III consortium should offer far more to certain faculty. If one is teaching at a "developing" college, he has the opportunity to become enriched through contact with the "developer" of his institution. Enrichment can include access to other faculty, resource material, and superior plant. Frequently much is lost in the transition from theory to practice. Three major factors combine to obstruct the cross-pollinating process: the distances between campuses, traditional autonomy, and the very nature of Title III grants—in that these monies are channeled to the individual institutions for theoretically, but not necessarily, cooperative programs. With no real incentives for collaboration, and no deterrent to noncollaboration, most faculties pursue the course of least resistance—inaction. To the degree that institutions view the Title III monies as income, the faculty and the consortium become competitors. The administration serves as an apportioning agent to both groups, and if the consortium's status in the campus hierarchy is quite low, it may expect to receive only the acceptable minimum. The remainder, quite often, is spent in a manner counterproductive to cooperation—for example, to strengthen a hitherto weak disciplinary structure. In other words, faculty do not necessarily view the Title III consortium as a vehicle for intellectual and programmatic enrichment, but rather as another outside source for badly needed maintenance budget funding.

The cooperative consortium usually involves the faculty to a far higher degree than do either service or Title III consortia. Some feature sophisticated operations, such as joint appointments or even departments, which institutionally require cooperation and commitment to the consortium by the affected faculty member. The administration's financial commitment to the consortium is an omnipresent factor. Such consortia, based on and in the member campuses, certainly offer far greater opportunity for faculty involvement which still has not happened in any substantial manner. Tradition has proved to be far stronger than any of the tangible or intangible rewards offered thus far. The faculty sense of loyalty to their discipline and to their department has far outweighed the challenge of developing an alternative system. Most schools find interdepartmental planning and cooperation extremely difficult, and interinstitutional planning and cooperation near impossible. The consortium, under suspicion by the faculty for being an outside influence to begin with, usually compounds this suspicion by proposing seeming radical programs—many cross-disciplinary, many cross-institutional. Such programs may be interpreted as a direct attack on the sanctity of the department, which, all things considered, is generally the core of the faculty member's professional life. Most faculty are defensive in their relations with consortia—they are likely to pay lip service to the principle of cooperation but strongly resist any attempts to involve their particular operation.

To those observing the consortia scene, there appears to be no sign of a natural, evolutionary development towards cooperation. If a consortium does its job, but waits for the faculty to come around, it may wait forever. If faculty involvement in cooperation is to develop to a significant degree, it must be accomplished by the consortium, for it won't be by inevitability. The basic tactical issue for the movement is that of seduction versus coercion. Seduction is considered by most consortia as the more appealing route, although, as a general rule, it has thus far failed. Much is said about money

—if we had it to use as a carrot, if we had enough to gain parity
with a department, if we had it to award, reward, promote, or
incite. This lack of money, however genuine, is to some degree an
idle excuse, in that the sums required will probably never material-
ize. But the problem is not as simple as finance. It is attitudinal.
Somehow it must be demonstrated that it is more prestigious to be
flexible, to cooperate, to innovate. The movement must commence a
monumental selling campaign if it is to get off the ground. It has
done a fair job with administrators, now it must tackle faculty. Such
a campaign can only be accomplished through an energetic and
total policy of inclusion. The faculty should be involved in the daily
decision-making and operating aspects of the consortium. A seat
on a program committee which meets semiannually is wholly insuffi-
cient—a continuous and broad-ranging demand on faculty time is
required. The faculty member should be knowledgeable in all aspects of the operations that affect him—from Academic to Xerox.
Only by coupling demand with flattery can the seduction route
succeed.

The easier short-run course is coercion, an option rarely
available to consortia. This won't win friends in the first generation,
but it has certain valuable attributes, among them: speed, clarity,
and the image of strength. Offsetting these attributes are the possible
alienation of long-time faculty members, the short-run trauma to
the institutions involved, and the effects of the immediate loss of
institutional identity on graduates, students, and faculty. Coercion
would appear feasible only in consortia composed of institutions in
the direst of straits, and, considering the enormity of the conditions
leading to such a situation, one wonders whether they could continue to survive even in drastically altered circumstances.

I can see no easy solutions for the issues of faculty commitment and participation. A "carrot-and-stick" approach is called for,
but how does one discover a series of "carrots," and how does one
develop an effective "stick"? These questions will remain unan-
swered for the movement as a whole because the movement is far
too diverse to permit any universal applications. But the "stick"
should be directed toward faculty involvement in a substantive role,
and the "carrot" should be benefits accrued through faculty participation in the decision-making process.

Role of the Executive Director. The executive director is the single key individual in the operation of any consortium. While there is no formal national mechanism for identifying, selecting, and training candidates for the chief executive position in consortia, the present consortium directors tend to have certain similarities. Though they range in age from the early thirties to the sixties, most are in their late forties and early fifties. Their educational backgrounds tend towards the humanities, with preparation in history not uncommon. In one way or another, they all were in positions of educational administration prior to their present appointments. Several were assistants to presidents of institutions; some were vice-presidents of colleges or universities; and others came from deanships and comparable positions. With some exceptions, they seem to see the executive directorship as the top of the ladder for them in educational administration. Some plan to hold the job until retirement while others look forward to returning to teaching. It may be significant that none appears eager to go on to bigger and better consortia.

Executive directors typically allow that they get along well with the presidents of their member institutions, but not with middle institutional academic management such as department chairmen and division chairmen. Almost none have a great deal of contact with students, and for many there is little contact with faculty members. All appear to attempt to avoid internal campus politics, but all wish they had more clout in affecting institutional orientation toward cooperation.

Most take pride in regular and rather constant travel to their member institutions, which, they feel, increases consortium presence at the campus level and develops and guides institutional participation in cooperative endeavors. The executive director in a large consortium sometimes resembles a circuit rider in his attempt to maintain the consortium presence on twenty or so campuses. In any case, most often it is Mahomet who goes to the mountain—the executive director characteristically plans conferences and major meetings on campuses rather than at consortium headquarters—a condition more due to lack of central space than his lack of desire for meetings on consortium ground.

By all odds, the telephone is the most valuable communication tool an executive director has. Telephone systems in current consortia range from two- or three-line push-button telephones to KCRCHE's elaborate "dedicated telephone network," involving two national WATS lines, an annual budget of approximately one hundred thousand dollars per year, and the ability to transmit computer data, telelecture instruction, and conferences among all the member institutions. The telephone proves to be a vital link in that it is rare that a director can poll, inform, cajole, or keep in touch with interested individuals at his member institutions as well by any other means. But in spite of the telephone seeming to be the logical, primary information transmitter for the executive director, it may be noteworthy how little the phones ring during one's visits to most executive directors. While the telephone is the primary available tool, it is not used for interinstitutional communication with a high frequency in the offices of many executive directors.

At times, a major factor in the direction and growth of a consortium is that each executive director—whether he admits it or not—feels closer to some institutions in his consortium than to others. His pet institution generally has one or more of the following characteristics: it is the institution from which the director came; it is close by geographically; it has a larger investment in the consortium than the other members; it is close (or home) for the consortium headquarters; its administration and the executive director have a personal kind of affinity. The new directions contemplated by an executive director may originate at or favor his favorite institution more than others. This is not necessarily bad, for the favorites generally have a far greater interest in and commitment to cooperation than do other institutions in the group.

Executive directors who were interviewed seemed to feel free to discuss and criticize other consortia but were quite reticent about being evaluative concerning the past experience of their own. Very few consortia have seriously studied themselves with an eye toward substantial reorganization or revision. Most executive directors are so caught up in current operations and so strapped both for time and money that the notion of substantial retrospective evaluation and forward planning seems realistically remote to them. A significant exception to this general rule, which also demonstrates the benefits that can be obtained from such evaluation and planning, is the self-study conducted by the College Center of the Finger Lakes. The impact of the study was due to its depth, exactness, and solid backup work, which had consumed the consortium's attention for over a year. But the full significance of the CCFL self-study does not lie in the report itself, although it is a comprehensive, informative document. CCFL's self-examination is principally significant because of the actions it triggered. The consortium membership read the report, understood it, and chose to implement it—at the expense of losing five institutions.

Unfortunately, most consortia as presently constituted can afford neither the time nor the expense of such studies—a condition which is a likely prescription for organizational mediocrity. Every executive director who was interviewed expressed a desire for grant support to make evaluation and forward planning possible. Such grants ought to be made available to consortia whose executive directors and boards would be willing to undertake seriously such examination, review, and redirection. Start-up or incentive grants are also needed to help establish the new directions, programs, and governing systems that emerge from such evaluative and planning reviews. Most cooperative arrangements do not have the manpower or the cash available to permit either self-study, significant innovations, or major shifts in emphasis, and this condition is acknowledged by executive directors. It should be a responsibility of federal funding sources, and perhaps private foundations, to acknowledge these needs and to consider how they may be met if the consortium movement is to advance as it should. Another substantial need for support exists in terms of the training and professional development of executive directors. Executive directors exhibit a refreshing humility about their own capabilities and an eagerness to improve their professional effectiveness in consortium leadership; they would welcome some guidelines, especially in the skills and concepts of governance and organization that enable consortia to move more effectively toward planned academic complementarity and the cooperative planning and operation of physical facilities. Private foundations and/or the federal government should invite the present loose association of executive directors of consortia to project a reasonable plan for such personal development and training over the next five years, and should consider significant grant support for such efforts.

Executive directors as people are good, solid men and women, almost uniformly convinced of the rightness of the basic idea of cooperation but suffering under severe handicaps placed on them by their situations. The feeling that nobody cares transcends most others exhibited by executive directors. One comes away from visits into the field with a vivid sense of their sense of frustration. No director is particularly happy, each wonders for the movement, all are sure things should be much better, but do not see how when faced with their present financial constraints. They feel impotent, and view money as the panacea. There is a universal feeling that the student is being short-changed. Most view their role as providing a vehicle for a greater educational experience for the student bodies they serve. Any failure of their consortium's programs is at the students' expense. On the other hand, they usually have little contact with the students, and one comes across few efforts to mobilize student support for consortium activities. Executive directors may be timid about following this route—that if they did they would be guilty of an assault on institutional autonomy which might alienate their presidents, perhaps causing the demise of the consortium or the termination of their own positions.

Most executive directors feel that faculty is the central issue following money, but there is a great divergence of opinion on how to relate to faculty members as a consortium factor. Most executive directors advocate avoiding the administrative end of their member institutions as much as possible but, paradoxically, appear to devote most of their efforts there. All their efforts are frustrated by an awareness that the usual consortium has little genuine standing on the member campus. The movement has very much of a "we-they" rather than "us" emphasis. The CCFL model is a valid attempt at breaking this, but the preponderance of money, power, and people will always lie with the member campus. The lot of the executive director is to be frustrated. His only tools are his charm and imagination, and his premier enemy is tradition, particularly the tradition of institutional autonomy.

Most executive directors feel that they are highly understaffed, and that this leads to a lessening of their potential. Staffing varies greatly among consortia, and there does not appear to be a good rationale for this divergence, except cash available. Executive directors of consortia visited in this study have staffs ranging from a half-time secretary to over sixty-five full-time employees. Operating resources—be they Xerox machines, postage meters, furnishings, or supplies—have also never approached the level enjoyed by the member institutions. It is almost as though there were an unconscious intent of the membership to remind the consortium that it is of lower caste than any individual institution. One is led to conclude that if a given consortium appeared to be gaining parity with any member institution, its membership would immediately overhaul its budget. The idea that one's consortium is rather like a mother on welfare—worthy, but incapable of self-sustenance—is understandable but unfortunate. While all directors stress their good relations with their presidents, it is obvious that they tend to view themselves, and tend to be viewed by the members, as second-class citizens. They appear to be ever apprehensive that no matter how much they do or how much they bring in, they are never quite acceptable. This particular frustration is virtually universal.

Perhaps this is the main reason for the high turnover rate among executive directors. Certainly some leave because of the frustration of the second-class academic citizenship. The remainder who leave are fired. Consortia are viewed by the members like baseball teams: If things are going badly, you don't look at the players, as it were; rather you fire the manager. This simplistic view appears to have doomed many an eager director and perpetuated many a mediocre consortium.

Thus the governance of contemporary consortia of colleges and universities reflects the surviving strength of institutional autonomy. Even where it may not be appropriate, governance lies principally in the hands of institutional presidents, who may or may not have strongly favorable convictions about the advantages of interinstitutional cooperation. The problem of developing a commitment to academic complementarity and other cooperation on the part of member institutions is clearly the central issue in effective governance. If this commitment does not exist in a substantial sense, no system of consortium organization, simple or complex, will assure effective operation. If the commitment exists, a consortium needs to determine whether it wishes to be service-oriented or cooperation-oriented, and then it should establish a form of governance suited to its needs.

The governance of a service consortium should at the very least be centralized at the headquarters and be directly controlled by those who have the highest stake in developing financially viable service programs of high quality. This control may be realized best by an independent, self-governing, nonprofit or profit corporation contracting to serve institutions.

In contrast to the service consortium, the governance of the cooperative consortium should be rooted firmly in its participating institutions. It is thus logical and necessary for the board of a cooperative consortium to include the chief executive officers and trustees of participating institutions. In addition, the cooperative consortium would benefit by forms of governance and management that help to insure the diffusion and encouragement of consortium leadership and management at the participating campus level as well as at a central headquarters.

The consortium movement today has a long way to go to strengthen the forms of governance of either service consortia or cooperative consortia. Significant grant support is needed to provide retrospective evaluation and adequate forward planning; similar grant support is seriously needed to enable the upgrading of executive directors. Both kinds of support might help assure that a continuing movement toward interinstitutional cooperation will justify itself in terms of quality.

Chapter 5

THE CONSORTIUM OBSERVED: FIVE EXAMPLES

It helps one gain a sense of the movement to look in some detail at individual consortia. To that end, this chapter presents profiles of five cooperative groups of colleges and universities in several parts of the country. Only one—TAGER in Texas—may be thought of as notably radical in terms of its approach to the cooperative delivery of educational services. The others—Union of Independent Colleges of Art, Colleges of Mid-America, New Hampshire College and University Council, and Greensboro Tri-College Consortium—are relatively unexceptional in their approach to academic cooperation and interinstitutional service, and suggest therefore many of the parameters within which the movement tends to operate.

The Association for Graduate Education and Research (TAGER)

The campus of the University of Texas at Dallas is located on the northern edge of the metropolitan area of that city in fairly open country. The Dallas branch occupies several hundred acres of undeveloped land, and has only a few buildings, one of which is the TAGER headquarters. The TAGER building is unpretentious, a single story in height, almost dwarfed by the high microwave tower that stands beside it. There is little about the site or the outside of the building to suggest the headquarters of what one distinguished educator (Killian, 1972) has called "the outstanding example in this country of an industrially sponsored educational system for promoting the advancement of in-service employees in companies . . . and for serving educational needs at the campuses of a number of colleges and universities." With little flamboyance but with considerable effectiveness and promise, TAGER's operations from this nerve center constitute a unique phenomenon in the consortium movement.

The University of Texas at Dallas has few students, all of them at the graduate level. Texas does not plan to put the Dallas campus into larger scale operation until 1975. This branch of the university is an outgrowth of an earlier establishment on the same site, the Southwest Center for Graduate Studies, which was a private, nonprofit research and development institution founded in the late 1950s at the initiative of senior executives in Texas Instruments and other high-technology enterprises in the Dallas area. The same people who founded the Southwest Center for Graduate Studies were later prime movers in the founding of TAGER.

The middle 1960s was a hothouse period for technological development as well as higher education everywhere in the United States. The Dallas-Fort Worth area witnessed a major expansion in the development of high-technology industries but had very little strong graduate scientific and technological education except for what existed at Southern Methodist University. TAGER was originally conceived in this hothouse to provide for better and easier access to graduate education in science and technology, both for regular graduate students and for students employed in industries around Dallas. Among educational institutions, the principal initiative for the establishment of TAGER by state charter in 1965 were Southern Methodist University, the Southwest Center for Graduate Studies, and Texas Christian University. On the industrial side, leadership was given by three principal figures, all from Texas Instruments: Cecil H. Green, Erik Jonsson, and Eugene McDermott. These men and institutions were enthusiastically interested in enlarging graduate education in science and technology for the area, and saw TAGER as an instrumentality which could help this happen.

At the very beginning, it was not conceived that TAGER would be principally a television-based instrumentality, but that it would operate as an educational consortium very much like most of the interinstitutional groups in the country. It began with seven private institutions, and attempted to provide for interinstitutional cooperation and instruction and in-plant instruction, by transporting either students or faculty members or both. But it was recognized very early by those associated with TAGER that transportation among a widely dispersed group of institutions and industries was not the most productive way to provide for interinstitutional cooperation in instruction. Largely because of the initiative of the men from Texas Instruments, consideration was given to the possible uses of television as a means of delivering instructional service to the educational consumer without transporting students or faculty members.

Planning for television-based instruction began in the fall of 1966 under great pressure, and the TAGER system became operative on television in September 1967. During that year an organization for academic coordination among associated institutions was established, a video and audio system was devised, and a central engineering and switching facility was built on the Dallas campus. The central facility at Dallas today includes office space, an engineering and technical studio, and the three-hundred-foot microwave relay tower. Affiliation with TAGER is now held by nine colleges and universities, including two state-supported ones: Austin College, Bishop College, Dallas Baptist College, Southern Methodist University, Texas Christian University, Texas Wesleyan College, The University of Texas at Dallas, The University of Texas Southwestern Medical School, The University of Dallas. In addition, the following industrial plants participate in TAGER: Atlantic Richfield, Bell Helicopter, Collins Radio, General Dynamics, LTV Garland, LTV Grand Prairie, Mobil Oil, Sun Oil, Texas Instruments–Dallas, Texas Instruments–Sherman.

TAGER's principal benefactor has been Cecil H. Green. Mr.

Green contributed approximately one and a quarter million dollars to the establishment of TAGER and has served as chairman of its board of trustees. His gifts were approximately one-half of what it took to establish TAGER; the other half was provided by institutional spending to create TAGER facilities on their own campuses and by industrial financing of facilities and microwave links for the system. TAGER is currently operating in the black on an annual budget of a little over two hundred thousand dollars.

TAGER's principal means of achieving its educational goals is the Green Network. This is a microwave educational broadcasting system designed to bridge electronically the distances that separate participating institutions and industries in the Dallas-Fort Worth area. Microwave circuits, permitting both educational program initiation and educational program reception, now interconnect all nine colleges and universities; participating industrial firms have created microwave interconnections with the Green Network and in-plant receiving classrooms to serve the educational needs of their own personnel. The multichannel microwave "spine" of the system now runs from Southern Methodist University in Dallas, via TAGER, to Texas Christian University in Fort Worth. Radiating microwave spur channels interconnect all other institutions and industries.

In addition, TAGER operates four channels of microwave broadcast coverage from its headquarters to cover effectively the entire city of Dallas without the need for dedicating a special channel for each prospective user. Two such channels are also in operation in the Fort Worth area. While serving in a "broadcast mode," these channels actually operate at very high frequencies (designated ITFS) especially reserved by the Federal Communications Commission for educational television. Reception on the ITFS channels is not possible by the customary commercial television receiver without special facilities and electronics.

In December 1972, TAGER initiated a new dedicated circuit on a special channel interconnecting the University of Texas Health Science Center at Dallas with five hospitals in the Dallas area for a variety of medical and paramedical training courses. TAGER is also undertaking a cooperative library center serving all of North Texas through computer interconnection. This would provide central union catalogue and other services to college, university, and other libraries of the area.

R. C. Peavey, a scientist and science administrator, came to TAGER in August 1969, as director. He succeeded two earlier directors who had served relatively short terms of office. Dr. Peavey had been associated with the Southwest Center for Graduate Studies prior to coming to TAGER, and before that he had been on the staff of the National Academy of Sciences in Washington, D.C. His associate director, Lee Crandell, is in charge of technical and business operations of TAGER, and came to the consortium from Collins Radio, with long experience in electronic development and a master's degree in electrical engineering.

During the last half of 1972, Peavey served as interim executive director of the Inter-University Council of the North Texas Area (IUC) as well as executive director of TAGER. His doubling up of duties represented a first tentative step toward consolidation of the IUC and TAGER. While actual consolidation had not taken place by the end of 1972, the two organizations were being served by one administrative office headquartered at TAGER. The IUC is a large, relatively loose consortium including the following institutions: East Texas State University, North Texas State University, Southern Methodist University, Texas Christian University, Texas Woman's University, The University of Texas at Arlington, The University of Texas Southwestern Medical School, The University of Dallas, Austin College, Bishop College, Dallas Baptist College, Texas Wesleyan College, Baylor College of Dentistry, The University of Texas at Dallas.

Although the purposes of the Council are essentially synonymous with those of TAGER, in general terms, IUC has undertaken only a few very limited cooperative academic efforts. The IUC principal success has been in interinstitutional library loans, a private-line teletype system and daily courier to speed exchange of library items, a common library courtesy card for faculty and all graduate students in constituent institutions, and a document exchange program for surplus library materials, mainly periodicals and serials.

Within TAGER, there is no current system of free interchange enrollment of students of the kind in Five Colleges, Incorporated, the Worcester Consortium for Higher Education, and certain other groups. Instead, TAGER operates among its institutions by cross-listing courses or providing for teachers who are offering TAGER courses originated at one campus to be recognized as adjunct professors on the other participating campuses. A student enrolls at his own institution or industry in a TAGER course, no matter where it originates, his course is recognized and given credit by his own institution. For each enrollment in a course offered elsewhere, the receiving institution is charged one hundred dollars. This amount passes through the consortium central headquarters and is returned to the originating institution as income.

The membership fee for each senior (large) institution is ten thousand dollars a year; for small institutions it is five thousand dollars per year. In addition, each participating institution, regardless of size or number of classrooms involved in TAGER course work, is charged twenty-five hundred dollars a year for maintenance and operation of the system. Participating industries are charged for the numbers of channels they use and for maintenance and operations costs.

Since September 1971, the pricing structure of TAGER course offerings has been based on what Peavey calls the "time-slot concept." This means that, in addition to all other fees, TAGER sells three-hour semester course time for six hundred dollars to any participating institution. At one hundred dollars per student, the sending institution then needs an enrollment of at least six off-campus students to break even against the six-hundred-dollar time-slot charge. This time-slot pricing system applies equally to private and public institutions in the TAGER consortium. Public institutions keep both their time-slot charges and the student income money in an escrow account at TAGER headquarters, in order to keep these monies from becoming entangled in the regular financial bureaucracy of state institutions. Industrial courses are charged at a rate of one hundred dollars per course hour.

By 1970, some two thousand students were enrolled in semester courses in TAGER. While TAGER was initially begun to serve the educational needs of industrial personnel in the area, nearly half of the TAGER semester enrollments by the fall of 1971 involved students on the participating campuses. In the spring term of 1972, total semester enrollments in TAGER had fallen to the neighborhood of sixteen hundred. This apparently reflected two things. One was the impact of industrial cutbacks in space, related technological contracts, and layoffs and readjustments, which reduced the demand for graduate education for employees. The second factor tending to depress TAGER enrollment by the spring of 1972 may have been the pricing structure. Institutions, like industries, were affected by economic considerations, and did not necessarily see TAGER cooperative course work as a vehicle for economizing. The future for TAGER is thus unclear. The colleges and universities involved have not yet addressed vigorously the possibility that TAGER course offerings, if expanded, could enable significant savings for individual institutions. This is regrettable because TAGER demonstrates vividly many of the advantages of telecommunications in the delivery of educational service over a wide area.

The technology that TAGER uses is highly simplified, economical, and easy to use. Not only does it provide for excellent video and audio transmission to all receiving institutions and industries, but, most important, it also provides for simultaneous easy audio interaction between instructors and students. Another great virtue and strength of the TAGER operation is its total dependence on live communication; almost no recorded material is used. Students are in touch with instructors electronically in real time, and the psychological quality of the learning situation has much of the sense of actuality, improvisation, and humanness that one finds in a regular classroom.

Early on a March morning in 1972, I went to the campus of Texas Christian University at Fort Worth to sit in on TAGER course work. I was met at the local campus TAGER building by Richard F. Raeuchle, deputy for TAGER at TCU. Raeuchle is a professor of physics and spends approximately one-half of his time supervising the TCU TAGER unit and coordinating TAGER operations on his campus. He reports directly to the dean of the graduate school.

In the TCU TAGER building I was shown two receiving classrooms in operation, plus a sending classroom studio. The receiving classroom had space for twelve students; all of the space was taken by TCU undergraduates. One of the courses I observed was in calculus, given by a mathematics professors at Austin College, some distance to the north of Dallas. The TCU students were in two-way audio communication with the professor at Austin via telephone interconnection, carried on multiplex over the TAGER microwave system. The professor at Austin began the class by taking roll, calling the name of each student at all participating campuses. Those at TCU answered by picking up the telephone next to their seats and responding. Thereafter, the course continued very much as in a regular classroom, except that the professor was available to the students only through the audio system and the video tube. Students responded to questions the professor posed and asked questions of their own by telephone. After the first few minutes, it all seemed very easy and natural. The students I spoke to seemed to feel that it was a useful way of getting the particular calculus course that the professor from Austin was offering.

Raeuchle then showed me the classroom sending studio, which was well yet simply equipped. The sending studio seats twenty-four students for live instruction, has two fixed television cameras at the rear of the room, and one fixed television camera directly above the table at which the professor sits. The overhead camera continually scans the table top before the professor and is capable of picking up charts, diagrams, or any other material that he presents or draws in connection with his teaching. Immediately behind the sending classroom is a control studio with three monitoring screens, one for each camera. Ordinarily during instruction the monitoring screens are handled by student operators who switch from one screen to another in accordance with the desires of the teacher. If the professor is talking directly to students either in the classroom or on the network, one of the two fixed cameras in front of him transmits it. If he desires a visual demonstration of material he is presenting, the student operator picks up the vertical camera on screen. In addition, the three screens are continuously monitored at the central switching studio at TAGER headquarters at Dallas, so if the student operator is absent or not alert to changes needed, or if any one of the cameras is not operating adequately, the central monitoring can make corrections. Because the cameras are fixed, there is no requirement for actual cameraman operation; the system is simply switched on and begins operating. The simplicity and economy of the classroom technology are impressive. This means that there is not a lot of subtle or creative camera work done, but it also means that the whole operation is very straightforward and easy to manage. According to Raeuchle, the studio classroom was used approximately 50 percent of the spring of 1972; he estimated 100 percent use in the academic year 1972 to 1973.

Part of the live quality of TAGER instruction results from the instructor not being away from the actual physical presence of students. While teaching students far away via the TAGER system, he is also teaching students directly with him in the sending classroom. The result is that the teaching one sees on TAGER is not canned but much like what one sees in most good classrooms.

On the debit side, there was little promotion of TAGER courses on the TCU campus, in spite of the chancellor's strong interest in TAGER cooperation. This may reflect a lack of imagination in TAGER and campus leadership more than a failure of central administrative enthusiasm. There is not much done aside from regular catalogue announcements and occasional stories in the campus newspaper. And although the TAGER facility at Texas Christian was built especially for TAGER operations and is new and attractive, I was surprised at how small it is. While TAGER exists and operates well, participating institutions like Texas Christian have only just put their toes in the water of consortium participation.

Having seen what TAGER can do in small, one hopes that the participating institutions will take much more advantage of what has been created than they yet have done. In a real sense, TAGER has broken ground for the possible creation of a remarkable new cooperative electronic educational community in North Texas. Its five years of operation have demonstrated its workability and basic economy. What remains to be seen is whether the colleges, universities, hospitals, and other institutions in North Texas as will have the imagination to reorder their educational processes and allocation of resources to take optimum advantage of this new system.

Union of Independent Colleges of Art (UICA)

Headquartered in offices at the Kansas City Art Institute, the UICA is notable as a national consortium of a small number of specialized institutions, remarkably effective in addressing itself to a limited number of common concerns of its members.

The leader of UICA at the staff level is Dean E. Tollefson, a vigorous, intelligent, engaging man, who works energetically for his own consortium and to advance the movement generally. When I visited Dean Tollefson in Kansas City, he was fresh from a long-range planning committee session of representatives from four of the UICA institutions. His active and sanguine temperament seemed to go well with the kind of institutional group he serves: a widely dispersed consortium of colleges of art that sense they have much to gain from a combination of essential collaboration and healthy competition.

The eight-year-old consortium includes eight colleges and institutes from California, Cleveland, Kansas City, Maryland, Minneapolis, Philadelphia, and Rhode Island. These are all professional schools, accredited by their respective regional accrediting associations as well as by the National Association of Schools of Art. As an academic consortium, UICA's stated goal is to advance the professional work of its constituent members, their faculties and students. UICA's operations are supported by annual contributions of member institutions, by modest private foundation grants, and by Title III money that accounted for over half of the consortium income for 1970–1971.

In serving its members, UICA tries to improve communication among them on matters of common concern, to create joint programs as needed, to develop new educational materials and resources, to encourage research in art and design education, and to secure funding. It does at least some of these things very well. One of its most interesting aspects is its support of interinstitutional curriculum development. During each of the years of its existence, UICA has concentrated cooperative curriculum development efforts on a single chosen area. These areas have included graphic design, painting and sculpture, the liberal arts, and other programs. During each year, selected faculty members meet from throughout the consortium, review their existing curricula, and plan in common for revised or new programs. If there is a chance for genuine academic complementarity to be achieved by the consortium, it will probably be as a result of this concentrated, collaborative attention to the improvement of given curriculum areas.

Several other programs of UICA are impressive for their practicality. One of these is the UICA Learning Resources Exchange. Books and other holdings in each of the institutions have been surveyed and catalogued, with information about them for the entire consortium made available through the library at each institution. In addition, there are easy procedures for interinstitutional borrowing and distribution of reproduced essential materials. For example, each member's library has audiotapes of the presentations and lectures made by distinguished visiting artists at the Minneapolis College of Art and Design. From another source, each member institution has been provided by the Exchange with a set of two hundred forty original slides using natural objects to demonstrate eighteen different principles of design. As each UICA member generates specialized materials of these kinds, new learning resources can be reproduced and made available to the whole consortium.

Students as well as learning materials move from one institution to another with relative ease. UICA's Student Mobility Program is especially adapted to today's students, and perhaps particularly those in the fields of art and design. Under the program, a student can attend another UICA institution for a semester or longer while remaining enrolled at his own college, receiving full credit toward his degree for the work completed there. In 1969 the consortium developed a Mutual Application Plan by which prospective students can apply to two or more of the UICA colleges using only one basic set of application credentials. In addition to this cooperative simplification of application procedure, UICA institutions jointly make their capabilities known to some thirty thousand high schools. By presenting themselves to prospective students as a group of institutions with many diverse capabilities, the UICA colleges give high school counselors and students a helpful view of what is available in art and design education in key places across the whole country.

The things that UICA is doing in faculty development, in collaborative business operations, and in cooperative financial development do not seem as notable as the programs touched upon above. The unpretentious operation of UICA is convincing, however; observation at the institutional level gives credence to Dean Tollefson's comment (1972): "The institutions in this consortium have needs which are very clear and on which they are at work. Their consortium relationship is proving to be a vitally important resource in meeting their needs. Their common objectives, as special-purpose institutions, have helped advance their joint work. Their capacity for interreliance is growing and their ability to rely on available expertise—without each having to invent the wheel again—is increasing. . . . A special facet of interreliance is the development of complementarity in academic offerings among the consortium institutions. To say that we cannot be all things to all people is trite, but to effect a working alternative to that circumstance and build access to emerging student needs and faculty interests through viable and continuing interdependency—that's the objective!"

Colleges of Mid-America (CMA)

One finds the headquarters of CMA on the fourth floor of the Insurance Exchange Building in Sioux City, Iowa. There a small staff headed by Everette L. Walker serves a consortium of six Iowa colleges and five South Dakota colleges. Like other consortium headquarters, the CMA offices are spare to the point of being Spartan. They have the air of a solid but not very prosperous insurance agency one might find somewhere else in the same 1920's building. The office windows look out on the barren pavements and older buildings of unthriving downtown Sioux City.

The consortium's executive officer carries the title of president of CMA. A good organizer and steady administrator, Walker is the second head that the four-year-old consortium has had. He was assisted by one other professional at the time of my visit, Robert McCleery, a young middle-aged educator with special interests in student personnel work. These two men, with secretarial assistance and considerable help from the participating campuses, administer the cooperative affairs of eleven small, mainly denominational colleges scattered across the flat prairie country from Huron, South Dakota, in the northwest to Storm Lake, Iowa in the southeast.

CMA began as a consortium officially in August 1968. But well before that time there had been stirrings of cooperation among these prairie colleges. Wendell Halverson (1972) remembers that when he became president of Buena Vista College in 1961, he was immediately welcomed into informal meetings with the presidents of Morningside, Westmar, Northwestern, and Briar Cliff Colleges.

A cooperative faculty workshop was held in Sioux City in 1963, and early in 1964 the Colleges of Middle America brought together certain colleges from North Dakota, South Dakota, Nebraska, Kansas, and Iowa, but this venture, although successful, was not continued a second year. Late in 1967, President Palmer of Morningside College hosted a meeting of several colleges, at which other consortia were discussed. On January 1, 1968, a committee drew a plan for the consortium that exists today.

Almost simultaneously with these events, others in the same group of colleges also were reaching toward the formation of a consortium. In December 1966, under the chairmanship of John Van Valkenberg, assistant to President Palmer of Morningside College, there were discussions about ways to obtain Title III funds. In this connection, a formal organization to be called the College Association of Northwest Iowa (CANWI) was suggested in June 1967. In March 1968, Sister Jordan Dahm, President of Briar Cliff College, expressed concern that *two* consortia were emerging with overlapping memberships. A merger of the two efforts resulted in the summer of 1968.

These colleges share an emphasis on liberal arts in the context of the Christian faith, an interest in focusing attention on the individual student, a desire to enrich programs, and a recognition of comparative strengths and relative weaknesses which could benefit and be benefited by cooperative effort (Halverson, 1972).

The planners of the CMA merger in 1968 spoke of possible areas for cooperation in academic fields, extracurricular areas, financial development, and public relations. It was thought that a cooperative program would require an executive with a small staff and an average contribution from each institution of approximately three thousand dollars a year. The founders assumed that "foundation resources could be found to supplement program areas," and that a beginning could be made "with a few manageable areas," developing "slowly but confidently as experience and good judgment lead us" (Halverson, 1972).

Looking back four years later (1972), President Lars I. Granberg of Northwestern College remembered that discussions centered on raising funds more effectively and cooperating to operate more economically. Early aspirations included enriched educational programs, faculty association and interaction, forming a collective voice for the improvement of higher education, and "a cultural influence in our region of Mid-America."

Like other consortia, CMA's accomplishments are not world-shaking, and cooperation is handicapped by the inertia of institutional autonomy and other factors. But the presidents appeared to be trying to close with some of the issues of cooperation (Wells, 1972). This is what is most interesting about CMA; as member colleges face the problems of enrollment, isolation, and the difficulty of funding, their leaders turn more and more toward a conviction that part of their institutional salvation must lie in cooperation. They are not wholly sure about the dimensions cooperation should take, not sure about giving up autonomy, and certainly not sure about how to engage and orchestrate their constituencies in cooperative efforts. But they are trying.

Meanwhile, mainly undergirded by Title III funds and operating within a budget of approximately three hundred thousand a year, CMA has built up a track record of cooperative activities that signifies at least a beginning. In 1971 CMA revised its bylaws and clarified its organizational structure. Under the board of directors (eleven college presidents) the CMA president supervises four main areas, each with an interinstitutional council: academic deans, business managers, development directors, and student personnel deans. It is promising that the academic deans council is the best organized of these bodies, but none is yet in powerful operation.

Something of the distance academic cooperation still has to go in CMA is candidly reported in comments Everette Walker made in his presentation to the annual meeting of the CMA Board of Directors in 1972. His comments related to interinstitutional activity or the lack of it in some of the major academic disciplines:

> *Art.* Members have met a number of times with an elected chairman. They failed to get together on a student or faculty exhibition during 1970–71 and therefore did not use funds which had been available for them.
>
> *Business and Economics.* This group has been inactive until recently when they organized to develop a departmental seminar for the spring of 1972.

Education. A number of meetings have been held, but little self-motivation has developed. This is an area which could produce some fine results.

English. One of the most active groups is the English group. They have met more frequently and with a purpose or program. Good leadership and active participation of all members has produced good results.

History and Political Science. No efforts to organize in this area.

Foreign Language. This group has met faithfully and has had well-planned programs. This is the only group which has sponsored activities for others. They have served high school students and faculty in an interesting manner.

Music. The second Band Festival and Clinic was held last year, and another such program is scheduled for early May in 1972. This represents a good working relationship within this group [Walker, 1972].

One gains a sense that some of the CMA academic groups are meeting and some are not, but very little sense that substantive decisions about interinstitutional academic programs of consequence are being made.

The most concrete parts of the CMA program stem directly from Title III funding, and tend to be directed at helping "the developing institution" in conventional ways rather than promoting cooperative academic complementarity or joint administrative and budgetary planning. Title III regularly disburses money to colleges to give faculty members opportunity for graduate study. Similarly, faculty development seminars are held, with Title III funding and participation by teachers from various campuses in the consortium. An example is the Workshop for College Teaching directed by Morningside College, attracting sixty faculty members from several institutions. Nearly 42 percent of the annual Title III grant money disbursed to CMA participating colleges goes for national teaching fellowships. In addition, Title III funds support a central career counseling and placement service for consortium students, planning-programing-budgeting seminars for administrators in the consortium, a central consortium listing of instructional aids, and other activities.

Because of distance and other factors, student interchange enrollment is not significant.

One comes away from CMA with an impression of eleven
colleges, small and struggling, seeking but not succeeding in finding
much salvation through the kind of cooperation they have achieved
so far. Like other consortia of small institutions, CMA has tried to
augment its vision by bringing in outside consultants. The earnestness
of its presidents in hoping for help from cooperation is a matter of
record. Its organization is rational, its leadership is conservative and
responsible, and the amounts of money it has from Title III are
respectable. But there are no major breakthroughs being made. This
may be because of the wide dispersion and isolation of the eleven
colleges. They may be too small and too scattered, and too locked in
to the older pattern of going it alone, for planned academic complementarity and collective financial management to emerge.
Whatever the cause, CMA is not developing cooperative academic
programing, providing more efficient business operations on a joint
basis, adding electronic or other technological aids to instruction,
engaging in long-range joint institutional planning, coordinating a
joint approach to admissions and recruitment of students (who are
in very short supply at most of the institutions of CMA), or overcom-
ing institutional territoriality and competitiveness.

Further, the major public institution of the region, the University of South Dakota at Vermilion, which lies quite within the
geographic area of the consortium, is not a member. No real effort
seems to have been made to persuade it to join CMA. Even with its
wide geographic dispersion and interstate character, CMA could
benefit by having its eleven small private colleges in cooperative
interaction with the University of South Dakota. CMA could benefit
too by microwave interconnection among its campuses in order to
pool educational resources, reduce redundancy, and create an electronic community of its colleges.

Symptomatic of the need for better educational cooperation
among the institutions in CMA is the prevalence of small class size
in the eleven colleges. Everette Walker made a survey of class size
in April 1971: 468 classes had student enrollments of ten or less; of
these, 153 were at the freshman and sophomore levels, and 216 had
from one to five students. The persistence of these conditions after

four years of consortium operation underlines how far CMA has to go in more adequately realizing its stated purposes.

New Hampshire College and University Council (NHCUC)

It is hard to imagine a man more properly suited to the role of executive director of a collegiate consortium in the Granite State than Henry W. Munroe, the archetypically Yankee founder and moving spirit of NHCUC. Nor is it likely one would find a more vivid instance of the importance of executive leadership in shaping a consortium program. NHCUC is one of the most interesting, lively, and promising of the voluntary consortia, in good part because of Henry Munroe. A profie of NHCUC has to begin and end with him.

Described by one admirer as "a truly wonderful nut," Munroe is a young middle-aged pipe-smoking New Hampshireman who works at being a codger, in his job and out. Over the past six years, he has led in putting together a consortium worth knowing about. Ardent concerning NHCUC's strengths and weaknesses, his life is full of many other things as well. A historian by profession, specializing in American military leaders of the Revolution and of the Civil War his side interests include General Patton, New Hampshire politics, early American construction techniques, developing a new religion, canoeing, maple sugaring, mast making, fire fighting, writing a book about the evacuation of Dunkirk, having a strong opinion about everything under the sun, and casting his opinions in pithy Yankee aphorisms at every opportunity.

NHCUC is located on the second floor of a modest frame library building at Notre Dame College in Manchester, New Hampshire. Munroe's office is small and looks well used. Other members of the consortium staff have comparable offices surrounding a fairly commodious secretarial pool area. Nothing about the headquarters is plush or on a scale that pretends to be impressive.

Three professional staff members assist Munroe. Lynn G. Johnson, the associate director since 1969, is a young Yale graduate with degrees in theology from the University of Edinburgh and the Union Theological Seminary. His past includes a directorship in a black-white community council and work in intergroup relations in South Philadelphia writing for the *United Church Herald*. While a seminarian, he carried pastoral duties for short periods of time in two New York churches. From 1961 to 1963 Mr. Johnson taught English in the National College of Ghana in West Africa. William W. Barnard, with NHCUC for a two-year period under special grants to work on academic cooperation, came to New Hampshire from a deanship at Ohio Wesleyan University. Douglas W. Lyon, who holds an M.A. degree in political science from the University of New Hampshire, was a Ford Foundation teaching fellow from 1967 to 1969 and has had teaching experience at the secondary level and experience in residential administration at the University of New Hampshire. These three men, with Henry Munroe, are a team of consortium utility infielders who can play the outfield as well when they need to.

The member institutions of NHCUC include four Catholic, two state, and three private nonsectarian New Hampshire colleges and the University of New Hampshire—all of the degree-granting public institutions and nearly all the private institutions in New Hampshire. More than eighteen thousand students are enrolled in these institutions, with nearly half at the University of New Hampshire.

Prior to the founding of NHCUC in 1966, Henry Munroe was administrative assistant to the president of New England College at Henniker, New Hampshire. In that assignment, he says that he came to the conclusion that private higher education would be doomed without cooperation. Aware that funding could be secured for cooperative ventures under Title III of the Higher Education Act of 1965, Munroe drafted a proposal for the formation of a consortium and convinced a small group of New Hampshire college presidents that a consortium could work for the best interests of their individual institutions. With that and a year's leave of absence, Henry Munroe organized NHCUC, choosing Notre Dame College as the site of its headquarters. Title III money was secured and channeled through Notre Dame. NHCUC institutions committed themselves to assessments and service fees for what the consortium could provide them, and on January 1, 1966, the consortium officially began.

It is interesting to consider the sources of funding upon which NHCUC had depended during the years since 1966. From January 1, 1966 to January 31, 1972 (including commitments received for 1972 to 1973 and 1973 to 1974), NHCUC had total funding in the amount of $3,168,882: $173,000 from philanthropic foundations; $66,000 from corporations and corporate foundations; $2,456,878 from the government; and $473,004 from institutional assessments. It is worth noting that less than 6 percent of NHCUC funding has come from private philanthropic foundations, distinct from corporate giving, while more than 14 percent of the total funding of the consortium has come from institutional assessments. The substantial nature of government funding of this consortium is evident; without it NHCUC could hardly exist. NHCUC is genuinely a Title III consortium, although it also fits the descriptions of academic and service consortia.

Harold L. Hodgkinson, while engaged in a study of Title III and its results, was so impressed by the accomplishments of NHCUC, that he said among the consortia he felt were doing an excellent job, NHCUC "turned out to be far and away the best of the bunch" (Hodgkinson, 1972, p. 13). He went on to say that NHCUC has succeeded through cooperation in waging war on financial instability.

Hodgkinson describes the operations: "All routine and most major administrative tasks are carried out through the consortium. Library transports move books between campuses daily; joint course numbering allows frequent student exchanges; the four-one-four calendar, a marine sciences program, and various cultural programs are the other fruits of cooperation for these institutions. The schools are now committed to interdependence, and while the manifest function of this sort of cooperation is clear, some of the latent functions are as interesting. . . . As one example, religious institutions within the consortium have for the first time adopted a contemporary approach to education in these areas . . . without sacrificing institutional identity" (Hodgkinson, 1972, p. 13).

Positive action has produced results in academic cooperation, even if these are relatively modest. The chairmen of curriculum committees on the several campuses formed the Cooperative Academic Programs Committee (CAPC), staffed by William Barnard. This committee meets monthly, has funding to provide for its staff, and, thanks to a foundation grant, has discretionary funds to allocate to faculty members who undertake cooperative academic programs of an innovative kind. At the end of 1972, this committee had identified some four hundred courses in the consortium with enrollments of under ten each and was concentrating on what might be done to combine and rationalize such courses on a more efficient basis.

Student interchange enrollment among the colleges is administratively easy. The interlibrary loan system works well, and makes it at least theoretically possible for each student in the consortium to have access to more than a million volumes. A nearly complete coordination of academic calendars in NHCUC provides a structural base for potential academic complementarity. With the consortium computer network, even the small colleges have at least one terminal connected with computer systems at Dartmouth or the University of New Hampshire. Several hundreds of thousands of dollars have been invested in faculty development programs. Beyond this, NHCUC has initiated a joint purchasing system for consortium members, a joint financial aid office with centralized billing and collection, and a handbook of standard specifications for building contractors.

The severest critic of the accomplishments of NHCUC is Henry W. Munroe. Working with a board of directors made up of his presidents, Henry Munroe has not hesitated to criticize shortcomings in cooperation or to issue challenges. He pushes constantly on the obsolescence of the notion of institutional autonomy. But he knows that institutional autonomy dies hard. He comments that, to presidents and faculty alike, the college and the consortium are "like mother and mother-in-law: you love 'em both, but mother more!" When he is optimistic, Munroe feels that his constant pressure on institutional autonomy is yielding results, observing that "this consortium . . . is now at the point where they are willing to cast the dice in favor of an all-out assault on academic autonomy" (Munroe, 1971b). But he has moments when his optimism is not so high. He feels that faculty, especially department heads, fail to understand that cooperation is imperative, in their own self-interest and for the survival of their own institutions. He regrets what he calls the inadequacy of long-range planning in NHCUC and works hard to get funds and ideas to correct this lack. Above all, he is not afraid to raise a vision of possibilities, negative and positive for the constituencies he serves.

While Munroe recommends reconstructing previously conceived institutional and individual prerogatives of academic curriculum into a cooperative role, he admits that "cooperative ventures are superficial, or tangential at best to individual concern and to the academic viability of liberal education in general. He wants to create interaction among member faculties of several institutions to lead to a cooperative interdependence that could overcome the barriers of geography, inadequate physical facilities, limited finances, and general lack of quality and to thus develop economically feasible ways in which small colleges can maximize both the variety and quality of their cooperative offerings. "These are ambitious and even frightening challenges" (Munroe, 1971a).

Henry Munroe believes that the alternative to cooperation, at least for most of his institutions, is dissolution, and that hesitancy in moving toward cooperation will result in the erosion or extinction of his colleges. He believes that his concept of "a community of colleges," involving the surrender of individual autonomy to some significant degree would help his colleges survive, and survive at a level of quality which would benefit students more fully than do the current programs of the individual colleges.

For Munroe, the consortium is "a glorious dream." NHCUC is as effective as it is, and as promising, in good part because its executive director is not afraid to argue for the dream and work for its realization. In November 1972, NHCUC carried the argument for assistance to cooperation into the theater of New Hampshire state government. In a strong policy statement to the Post-Secondary Education Committee of the New Hampshire Legislature, NHCUC argued that the position of all higher education in New Hampshire is precarious and that the best route for the legislature to take is to encourage cooperation between the public and private institutions of the state.

Greensboro Tri-College Consortium (GTC)

GTC in North Carolina demonstrates many aspects of the movement in microcosm. Its members—Bennett College, Greensboro College, and Guilford College—are quite homogeneous in one sense. All are relatively small, private, church-related, four-year institutions which were following a no-hire–no-fire policy in 1972–1973. Each college is distinctly different from the others, however, and the differences are deep-rooted in long-standing tradition.

Bennett College was founded in 1873 by newly emancipated slaves and the Methodist Episcopal Church as a coeducational institution. Early in this century it became a college for black women and eventually expanded to a maximum enrollment of over six hundred fifty students. As the 1970s began, its enrollment was running well under this figure, in part because of the competition of northern schools, which recruited both its faculty and traditional clientele. It has been left with an older, more traditional faculty which is resistant to change. Its administrative system, too, appears to suffer from an academic hardening of the arteries. Its student-faculty ratio in 1971 was a little over eight to one.

Greensboro College was chartered in 1938 as Greensboro Female College and became coeducational in 1954. In 1971, 73 percent of its six hundred students were female. Affiliated with the Methodist Church, it has also suffered from recruitment problems and has a student-faculty ratio of about eleven to one. Its recruitment problem stems from the refusal of the church-related board of trustees to agree with twentieth-century patterns of morality and student life. A restrictive social code and geographic location have hurt the school in its competition with other colleges. The expanding state university systems in the Southeast have also been a factor, as Greensboro has always been a regional college, geared primarily toward elementary teacher and health-related education.

Guilford College was founded by the Society of Friends in 1837 and is the oldest coeducational college in the South. Its main campus bears a striking similarity to Haverford College, from which it has traditionally drawn its faculty. In 1971, its enrollment was 1757, of which 1148 (65 percent) were male. Its student-faculty ratio is about seventeen to one—in part because of trustee policy, which states that the college and all its departments must not run in the red. Guilford has a downtown campus for continuing education.

The GTC headquarters are in the basement of the Guilford downtown division, a classroom building of the brick and cinderblock institutional style of the mid-fifties. Even by the previously mentioned modest office standard for consortia, GTC is humble: a small office for the director, a smaller supply room, and a desk in the secretarial pool area for the rest of the staff—a part-time receptionist-typist who makes eighteen hundred dollars a year. The consortium pays a modest rental to Guilford for this space.

William Lanier, the director, is in his late forties and is a historian by training. He is a Purdue graduate and is the head of the Purdue alumni in the Southeast. He first taught at Wittenburg University and then went on to Guilford College as academic dean. Lanier had hoped to concentrate on curriculum development at Guilford, but was disappointed in this hope. He submitted his resignation as dean, and the president of Guilford persuaded him to try operating the consortium, whose preceding director retired in June 1971. When visited in May 1972, Lanier expressed much satisfaction with the academic year then ending and said that he felt he had learned more and done more in curriculum development in one year with the consortium than he had during the whole of his previous career. Lanier is on the executive board of the Greensboro Chamber of Commerce, participates in local political activity, and in his private life is developing a number of beach houses on one of the outer Cape Hatteras beaches.

He does not see himself as a career consortium man and has not been active in the movement. He has been in the field only a year or so, and the lack of a travel budget has prevented him from going to professional meetings. This insularity has enabled him to be free of some of the constraints felt by consortium career people and has been a factor in his development of GTC. Without any staff and without any formal or long-time history constraining the consortium, GTC and Lanier have become interchangeable and highly flexible.

Lanier oversees two separate and distinct operations: the consortium and the summer school. The summer school is viewed as a money-maker for the three institutions. Its profits are divided among the three colleges on a ratio proportional to the number of credit hours taken by summer students from each member institution. Teaching positions at the summer school are divided among the three faculties, and Lanier does not allow "repeaters," in an attempt to broaden faculty involvement in the consortium. The summer school sponsored two workships in 1971: one on teaching exceptional students, which was financed by the state, and one on Southeast Asian studies for secondary schools, financed by the state and the federal State Department. Under the dual accounting system of GTC, Lanier receives a stipend for overseeing the summer school; the balance of his salary is paid through the Title III funds for the consortium.

At present there is no annual institutional financial commitment to the consortium from its members. In their absence, Lanier would like to keep a portion of the summer school income for consortium activities. Lanier feels that such a distribution would be a tangible, ongoing symbol of commitment to cooperation by his member institutions.

Lanier (1972) identifies the following as the major programs of the consortium: full-time director, half-time secretary; one-third time library coordinator and one-third time secretary; clinical psychologist; shuttle-bus service for students and library materials five days a week from 8:00 A.M. to 5:00 P.M.; curriculum workshops in history, elementary education, physical education, and earth science with coordinated and shared course offerings; all advanced courses in French offered at one institution; all advanced courses in Spanish divided (not duplicated) among the three schools; Guilford sends all music majors to Greensboro College; Greensboro sends all political science majors to Guilford; Guilford sends special education majors to Greensboro and Bennett; chemistry and physics programs; summer school; some speaker and cultural programs; joint opening-of-school faculty meeting.

By May 1972, the consortium had dropped tuition exchange for student interchange, had adopted a standard course numbering system, and intended to use a joint calendar in the fall semester. The admissions departments were working toward joint recruiting in the North Carolina area, and the business managers had decided that joint purchasing was impractical. Among academic departments, speech and drama had reorganized to prevent duplication, the history departments had decided not to cooperate at this time, the mathematics departments were considering a joint computer program, and the elementary education departments were developing a joint Junior Semester of Field Experience in Greater Greensboro.

The three colleges have, in Lanier's opinion, been most successful in the field of library cooperation. Each college is developing a resource collection in its field of particular interest: international studies at Guilford, black women's studies at Bennett, and urban studies at Greensboro. The colleges coordinate their serials subscriptions and their general book purchasing to avoid duplication. They have established a joint catalogue and a fast book-delivery service. At both professional and nonprofessional levels, all library employees meet regularly, and the professional group meets regularly with all the public librarians in Greater Greensboro. GTC has applied for a grant to switch the cataloguing from the Dewey Decimal to Library of Congress system, and Lanier is hopeful that it will be funded.

Lanier is a believer in institutional studies. He devotes time to assembling accurate comparative figures and has found visual aids depicting these comparisons valuable when making presentations to presidents, deans, or faculty members. As an example, he used this analysis-comparison technique to show that the Greensboro College music department, with only fifteen majors in 1972 (out of a total enrollment of 468) accounted for 20 percent of faculty members. These figures essentially demanded that Greensboro recruit students from the other consortium members, incidentally enabling Guilford to curtail its music program.

When he had brought up the music situation without charts and sheets, he found the meeting invariably turned to a discussion of Greensboro's great tradition in music, its popularity, and its personnel (who are part of the Greensboro family). Equipped with the graphically presented comparative data, he was able to keep bringing the meetings back to the point at issue and secure a cost-effective arrangement.

When asked in an interview to list his priorities, Lanier cited several aims. His first priority is to convene the academic deans and curricula chairmen to review all teaching loads. He feels the most important item in post-secondary education today is teaching the faculty fiscal responsibility; and he hopes that the result will be more interdisciplinary cooperative programs. He also hopes to establish career-oriented majors. The traditional career majors at Ben-

nett and Greensboro are out of step with the job market; and graduates from all three are experiencing difficulty finding employment.
Other items mentioned in his priority potpourri include (1) a joint
committee on art to coordinate bookings for cultural events through
the student governing boards; (2) more work on public relations
and public affairs, including putting together a slide show on GTC,
seeking some program time for GTC on the local educational television station, and getting an article on GTC published in the Sunday
magazine of one of the local papers; (3) a policy of tuition remis-
sion from the three boards of trustees for faculty, staff, and spouses
for a free term at member institutions; (4) the incorporation of GTC.

Thus far there has been no real cooperation with the two
major public institutions in Greensboro: the University of North
Carolina at Greensboro and the North Carolina Agricultural and
Technical State University. Lanier feels that computer networking
could eventually be a vehicle toward such private-public cooperation. The only member of GTC with a computer is Greensboro College, and its equipment is too small to be of much educational value.
But the state institutions are quite well equipped. The GTC unit
would remain as a separate operation in any larger arrangement.

Lanier feels he gets along well with the presidents. He has
his greatest difficulties with the faculty establishment. He feels the
most effective way to deal with tradition and autonomy is through
the boards of trustees. When decisions are left to the presidents
alone, they suffer from intracampus political constraints. If the decision is made a trustee decree, however, the president may be home
free. Lanier tries to use the position of director as a leadership position—he proposes to his board, rather than being directed by it.

GTC is an example of what even small institutions with a
small consortium budget can begin to do. The consortium benefits
from having an executive director who has love for the colleges and
the area, an imaginative board, and the spirit to fight to get things
done. But there is much still to do before GTC realizes the full potential of interinstitutional cooperation.

The consortia sketched in this chapter are not the best
known and are not representative, but they suggest where some of
the real promise of cooperation tantalizingly lies—in the use of new

technology for the delivery of educational services, in some measure of rationalized academic program cooperation, in joint systems of recruitment, in cooperative curriculum development, and the like. They give, too, some notion of the part the executive director does or does not play, of what he is up against, and what—against the odds of traditional institutional autonomy—he may be able to achieve.

But still these and other consortia do not answer the basic question: How can they be made good enough to help institutions meet the challenging period they have now entered?

Chapter 6

REALITY AND POSSIBILITY

In the consortium movement it is as though we have had all along the blueprint for a cathedral but have thus far built only a tool shed. This is not to denigrate the present accomplishments of individual consortia but to underline the gulf between idea and achievement, between rhetoric and reality. The performance of consortia up to this point has not measured well against the real opportunities and needs that have existed in American higher education in the past several decades. The general failure of the movement to deliver significant academic complementarity or significant planned cooperation in capital outlay or significant attention to the operating economies that might be achieved through cooperation or any substantial long-range planning of change and development—together with the continuing preeminence of institutional autonomy regardless of the redundancy of results—reflects a major opportunity thus far lost by consortia in terms of higher education as it has been.

With this record, it may seem romantic to suggest a bigger role for consortia in the years of radical change that lie just ahead,

But the revolutionary period we have entered in higher education cries out for some functions consortia could perform well, beyond the business-as-usual that has occupied them and their institutions up to this point.

This chapter tries to suggest a bold vision of the future for consortia, in terms of what Nelsen (1972a) calls "entrepreneurship and innovation." With proper incentives and external challenge, and with institutional leadership able to see beyond nose range to the real possibilities that lie in confederation and cooperation, something more like a cathedral than a tool shed could be built through consortium activity. It is reasonable not to be oversanguine, but it is important to restate the revolutionary context of higher education at present and note at least some of the concrete, practical, socially needed functions that would be appropriate for consortia in that context.

Continuing Revolution

The end of the 1960s did not signal the close of a revolutionary period in higher education, only its serious beginning. The conflict between the older institutional model and a nonelite mass clientele remains with us as it will until adequate new models come into play. The conflict between limited economic resources and virtually unlimited educational needs or demands remains with us, as it will until we invent better solutions.

Out of these two basic continuing conflicts—and connected ones, such as the rivalry between the public and private sectors of higher education for students and funds, the clash between institutional autonomy and the need for interinstitutional cooperation and coordination, the discontinuity between archaic modes of instruction and the massive growth of a high technology of communication—there is quietly emerging a revolutionary situation in which education beyond the high school will be transformed.

As Lyman Glenny points out, higher education does not yet grasp the full meaning of the now relatively quiet revolution in its midst, and it is not doing nearly enough to accommodate itself to change. Here are some of the intensely impelling factors in the pres-

ent picture not yet being responded to effectively by educators, either in institutions or in consortia.

The first factor is a continuing pressure for rapid reform within the old institutional model to adjust it to students who are not by cultural preparation disposed to conform to directive teaching, external evaluation, or extrinsic rewards.

The second factor is a developing demand on the part of many in the population for alternatives to the old institutional model. This demand looks toward more or less radically new arrangements, usable by many more than those who are willing and able to enter our two-and four-year colleges and graduate schools. This impetus toward innovation is showing up most familiarly in widespread talk about the possibilities of adapting the Open University scheme of the British to American purposes and in the emergence of such new organizations as the University Without Walls, the Union Graduate School, Campus-Free College, and Walden University. A related development, which we in higher education are largely ignoring, is the rapid growth of proprietary and corporate industrial schools.

The third factor is a strong indication in most projections, like those of the Carnegie Commission, that we are in for an extended period of slow growth or no growth in the usual enrollment patterns of colleges and universities. While enrollments doubled from 1960 to 1970, they will increase by only one half from 1970 to 1980, with the prospect of zero growth from 1980 to 1990, and a one-third increase in the last decade of the century. The assumed corollary of these projections is severe competition among institutions for available students. But the profound implications of these projections have not sunk in, as far as institutional leadership is concerned, as witnessed in the continuing efforts of many colleges and universities to expand. It is also witnessed in their tendency to continue to go it alone without trying to respond to changed market conditions through cooperative recruitment and admissions procedures.

The fourth factor is a manifest trend for the proportion of state budgets devoted to higher education to level off or decline. Budgets for higher education in two-thirds of the states already are declining in relation to other commitments. Concomitant with this trend, and enforcing it, is a general move toward centralized budget control in state boards of higher education and other state coordinating bodies—a move which is more responsive to overall state budget management than to institutional desires for autonomy, prestige, or resources. The swift rise to power of state coordinating agencies in higher education is deeply symptomatic of the economic predicament of higher education and of the end of an era of free competition for available resources by autonomous institutions.

The fifth factor is a substantial trend, in the public as well as private sector, toward requiring students to pay or to pay back an increasing proportion of the total cost of their education. The rise in private tuition charges and the pressure toward increased fees at public institutions force students and their families increasingly to shop among educational opportunities for the best buy. New payback systems, such as that exemplified by the Yale experiment and by the idea of the Educational Opportunity Bank, may well enlarge the development of a free-market condition in higher education; student choice goes to the institution or program that appears to offer him the most education for the least money. Most institutions continue to operate as though they will be the choosers rather than the chosen, as though the doubling of enrollments of the sixties were not over for good. Few if any institutional groups have sought to respond to the emerging free-market situation by any collaboration or cooperation.

The sixth factor is a clear signal that salvation for higher education-as-usual is not going to come from any federal Big Daddy. Beyond what may have been achieved by the complex Congressional legislation of 1972, we should not expect any major new governmental aid in the foreseeable future. Sidney Marland, in his remarks after designation as the first Assistant Secretary for Education in the Department of Health, Education, and Welfare, articulated the administration position without much room for doubt. In fact, establishment of the Assistant Secretaryship itself would seem to be a move toward nearly cabinet-level management of the operations of the Office of Education and the new National Institute of Education (NIE). Whatever the specific outcome, further federal activity in regard to higher education will likely be low on largesse and high on accountability. An exception, possibly, is that Title III monies will become a permanent subvention, encouraging consortia to form and operate.

The intriguing additional possibility is that significant new federal initiative for change, through NIE and the embryonic ten-million-dollar authority for innovation in postsecondary education, may come into the picture. If that happens, federal leverage may help push us to a new perception of realities and possibilities and to experimentation that concerns itself with creating a future for higher education.

Work on restructuring the old and inventing the new in higher education is indeed the order of the revolutionary period we have willy-nilly entered. Even though consortia have not yet played a substantial part in reorganizing higher education, they could do so. For that possibility to be realized at all, it will take some doing. Needed are new elements of challenge and stimulus outside the colleges and universities, an understanding of the major needs and opportunities now before higher education in a revolutionary period, and a raising of the sights of institutional leadership beyond the at least partially obsolete loyalties of institutional autonomy. None of these three requirements is going to be gotten easily.

Major Innovation

In the continuing revolution of higher education there is need for intelligent leadership of development and change via groups of institutions. This leadership would have an impressive agenda:

The collective rationalization of economic operations should include ways to optimize the income base of institutions from student payments and other sources, ways to match educational program with student-consumer demands, ways to economize in operating costs, and ways to plan capital outlay with reference to carefully selected priorities and without redundancy.

The collective rationalization of academic operations should include ways to provide programs that are complementary rather than competitive, ways to adapt the old institutional model to new requirements of openness and flexibility, ways to encourage institutional and faculty self-renewal, and ways to increase quality and opportunity beyond the capability of the individual institution working alone.

The collective development of new modes and alternatives in postsecondary education should include ways to go beyond the old institutional model to new programs that are not necessarily campus bound or limited to students from eighteen to twenty-two years old, ways to utilize the available technology of communication more productively, ways to provide self-paced learning for students of widely varying backgrounds and abilities, ways to help faculty toward greater pedagogical effectiveness and redefinition of role (including more capability in the inductive and advising mode), and ways to create new curriculum designs and materials appropriate to the last quarter of the twentieth century. The agenda above is all too summary, but it may be suggestive of the need and opportunity consortia now have to participate in major innovations. The revolutionary period of educational development that has begun asks for the leadership and resources which interinstitutional groups, at least in theory, could bring.

The consortium movement thus far gives us little cause for optimism about the response to these needs for major innovation. The operations of consortia seem to ignore or dampen whatever innovative impulses may exist. The exceptions to this statement serve mainly to demonstrate the rule. As one executive director said to me, wryly: "We cooperate on the easy things." But there are voices in the consortium movement that are calling for innovation in more than "the easy things." One of these voices is that of William Nelsen of the Danforth Foundation, one of the most perceptive young leaders in the field: "Consortium leaders must be fully cognizant of the major new demands being made upon higher education and the directions in which colleges and universities are called upon to move. Consortia . . . are often in a unique position to lead— especially in areas such as lifelong learning, the Open University, teaching improvement, combining new curriculum with the best of the old, financial planning, and other areas. . . . Consortia cannot be satisfied to coordinate old models of higher education when important new models are being developed" (Nelsen, 1972a).

Nelsen believes that the potential for entrepreneurship and

innovation on the part of consortia exists in a number of developing areas in education. Since no bolder voice than his is being heard, it is instructive to note the areas in which Nelsen calls for consortium action:

1. *Curriculum:* The old and the new can be combined *through an ongoing mechanism to monitor course offerings (especially majors).* A number of colleges try in their cooperative arrangement to prevent undue overlap in academic programs, but no voluntary consortium has yet established a permanent body with the power to approve, disapprove, and generally oversee new course offerings. The Washington, D.C. Consortium has moved in this direction by attempting to allocate certain advanced level courses to particular institutions, but few other examples come to mind. Nelsen agrees with the Newman Report that leaving course coordination to a state agency alone might run the risk of stifling initiative, discouraging diversity, and introducing unnecessary politicization in higher education. Voluntary consortia can prevent duplication in course offering while at the same time encouraging variety and differences in approach.

2. *Teaching:* Most colleges and universities do little to provide programs for the improvement of teaching on their own campuses. Nelsen says: "Faculty who often may feel threatened by a program that evaluates and seeks to improve teaching on the home campus may be much more willing to take advantage of a consortium-sponsored program" (1972a). The Kansas City Regional Council for Higher Education and the College Center of the Finger Lakes both have attempted to provide programs for the improvement of teaching. Enough promise lies in their experience to suggest that consortia could innovate in this direction to good effect.

3. *Admissions and retention:* In a time of stabilized or declining enrollment for many institutions, consortia could help institutions to recruit and keep students and encourage effective collaboration between colleges and secondary schools. The Associated Colleges of the Midwest has established joint admission and single application procedures. Certainly a great deal more could be done to make use of common testing, interviewing, and other methods of student evaluation in order to provide better counsel to prospective students as they consider the several institutions of a consortium. A

group approach here would recognize in practical ways the developing "free-market" condition that institutions face with prospective students, and provide such institutions with more effective mechanisms for relating applicants to institutional possibilities. Consortia could then capitalize effectively on the advantages a student has in one institution of a consortium in comparison to a nonconsortium institution. Student course interchange and even exchange of students across institutional lines for a semester or longer can open up more possibilities for students themselves and at the same time help to insure that institutional capacity will be adequately used. College-high school interaction could be effected by a "consortium of colleges linked to a consortium of high schools" working together on "new models of high school-college transition, information exchange, curriculum development and coordination, counseling and recruitment" (Nelsen, 1972a).

In all of this, consortia could have a remarkable opportunity to innovate, and to strengthen the capability of individual institutions to select and serve students collaboratively.

4. *Educational opportunities:* As alternatives to the old institutional model develop, consortia of colleges and universities have an unusual chance to help shape the future of postsecondary education. But they are not yet taking the initiative. The collective resources of a consortium could insure the viability and practicality of some of the new alternative models that are appearing.

A consortium-wide external degree program, for example, would have the potential of producing a rich and varied educational experience, more so than a program organized without an interinstitutional base. Consortium faculty and counseling resources might be brought into closer contact with external degree students in a carefully planned educational network than would be possible outside of a consortium; students could receive more classroom experiences, individual counseling and tutoring, and access to other varied resources.

A regional consortium could, if it wanted to, blanket a specific geographic area with educational programs and services, especially if it were able to coordinate and expand continuing education and extension services. Nelsen observes: "The potential for 'bringing education to the people' could be realized by academic institutions agreeing on a plan whereby each college could stake out specific areas (either geographic or functional) in which to bring its services . . . coordinated with business, government, and other agencies—which in certain cases might perform the teaching function" (1972a).

5. *Financial and educational planning:* Cooperative educational planning across the board could define role and purpose for various types of colleges and reduce unproductive competition between institutions. This is precisely what consortia thus far have not done well. In the private sector, most institutions, in consortia or not, are still going it alone as far as educational planning is concerned. In the public sector, statewide control boards and planning agencies are moving swiftly toward centralized coordination. According to Nelsen, the role and purpose for various types of institutions can best be examined by individual institutions in a collective setting, rather than through centralized coordination. Whether or not his hypothesis is correct, it deserves testing, and this will only happen as consortium leaders take a visible initiative in this direction.

The whole matter of consortia initiative in financial and educational planning is crucial. Consortium leaders have been timid in demonstrating the potential financial savings that cooperative programing can bring. They have been equally timid in pressing for genuine cooperative academic planning about important things. On both counts, present and future conditions challenge consortium leadership to exhibit more active entrepreneurship and more substantial innovation.

Leadership

Initiative toward a bolder vision of consortia as change-agents in the present revolutionary period may result from a maturing leadership in the field, from legislatively mandated incentives that are now developing, and from outside leverage like that of the new federal undertaking called the Fund for the Improvement of Postsecondary Education. All three of these elements are stronger than they were several years ago, and perhaps suggest the possibility of a new era of enlarged effectiveness for consortia.

The most significant and potentially promising evidence of

a maturing leadership that may raise the sights and increase the impact of the consortium movement lies in the beginning of the American Association for Higher Education (AAHE) cooperative program. In 1972 AAHE received a three-year grant from the Danforth Foundation to help support services to existing interinstitutional programs and to explore the strengths and weaknesses of consortia. The cooperative program subsequently established at AAHE headquarters in Washington, D.C. was an extension and formalization of the services activities that had earlier been provided to the consortium movement by Lewis Patterson and others working through the Kansas City Regional Council for Higher Education. The cooperative program at AAHE is headed by Patterson, who is pressing forward to improve the quality in the movement. Significantly, AAHE is the only major national organization that offers representation under a single umbrella to faculty, administrators, trustees, and students from every type of institution. Because of the wide variety of constituencies and institutions in the consortium movement, AAHE offers a logical and potentially productive central base.

Whether AAHE can evoke and enable more dynamic leadership in the consortium movement, however, still remains problematic. The Danforth grant is modest; in response to the request for $117,795, the Foundation granted eighty thousand dollars: thirty-five thousand for the first year; twenty-five thousand for the second; and twenty thousand for the third. The foundation also made the condition that the cooperative program should make up the difference between $80,000 and $117,795 from other sources. Thus the new program at AAHE is not only modestly funded and on a short term, but its officers are urgently admonished by their situation to spend time seeking other funds. The cooperative program is thus underfunded and thereby handicapped.

Even so, this move has shifted the consortium enterprise—at least for a time—into a more established mode, attached to a national organization of consequence which is itself change-oriented. The move also means that, at least modestly, the interconsortium services earlier provided informally by Lewis Patterson and others have somewhat more solid ground on which to stand.

The services presently provided by the cooperative program

at AAHE reflect both the limitations and the potential contributions that may be expected in this new phase. They include (1) editing and publishing *The Acquainter Newsletter* (ten issues per year), *The Consortium Directory* (annually), *Consortium Seminar Papers* ('semiannually), a *Comprehensive Bibliography on Cooperation* (periodically), a *Summary Report on Consortium Research,* and other occasional papers; (2) continuing to develop an information resource center including files of data on individual consortia, consortium literature, government and agency research reports directly related to consortia and cooperation, data on consortium positions open and vitae on available personnel, and data on persons and professional groups available for consultation; (3) referring interested individuals, institutions, and agencies to exemplary consortium programs and assisting in planning consortium visits; (4) assisting consortium personnel to contact governmental agencies, foundations, and representatives of national educational organizations; (5) encouraging and enabling cooperation and exchange of information among consortia, particularly those programs which have resulted in institutional savings; (6) exploring and encouraging cooperation between consortia and state coordinating agencies, including the Education Commission of the States and the three interstate compacts; (7) assisting consortium personnel and consortium *ad hoc* committees in arranging for national meetings, acquiring speakers, and making other arrangements; (8) conducting and reporting on limited research projects; (9) supporting and calling attention to the voluntary cooperative movement in general; and (10) being available for general consultation.

This list of functions is very heavily loaded on the side of services internal to the consortium movement itself. In reasonable reflection of its limited financial and staff situation, the activities of the cooperative program specify very little with regard to entrepreneurship and innovation, and thus it is unlikely that dramatic initiative for major innovation in the consortium movement will emerge from the cooperative program of AAHE in the three years of Danforth Foundation support. The establishment of a national service base for the movement may, however, provide a platform on which more dynamic leadership may stand and from which it may be heard.

Other private foundations have played a part, although not often a major one, in the history of the consortium movement. Several have made impressive efforts to aid and guide interinstitutional cooperation, both in general and in connection with particular consortia. The Ford Foundation, for example, has given very substantial support to the Atlanta University Center, perhaps enough to provide that consortium of six institutions with the momentum and strength of a major cooperative force in southern education. The Danforth Foundation has had a continuing interest in the consortium movement.

For the most part the consortium movement has not attracted heavy support from the private foundation world. Foundation executives tend to be skeptical about the substantive effectiveness of current interinstitutional cooperation. Consortia appear to foundations as more shadow than substance. Their rhetoric is seen as outrunning the reality of their academic and financial cooperation. The relative absence of private foundation influence on the consortium movement at present is a result of a low level of support. This may be regrettable because the movement is apparently here to stay for the foreseeable future, and it is still formative. Operating costs of consortia certainly should not be seen by anyone as the responsibility of private foundations, but this does not warrant a conclusion that selective grants to consortia—designed to stimulate them and provide concrete incentives in the direction of significant academic complementarity and fiscal planning, and to encourage programmatic entrepreneurship and innovation—would be inappropriate. The reverse is true. The meagerness of consortium resources, the critical problems faced by many participating institutions, and the great willingness of many executive directors to do more than they are now doing, combine to create a situation in which private foundations could exercise very influential leadership on the movement. Whether they will do so or not remains to be seen.

Perhaps the pressure for a bolder role for consortia will come from legislative and other action by state government. A sign pointing in this direction is the Education Cooperation Act (1972) of the Illinois State Legislature and the House Bill 4528 which proposed the act is something of a landmark. For the first time, in any explicit and substantial way, a state government was directed to provide financial incentives to programs of interinstitutional cooperation in higher education. The bill called for a program of financial assistance to consortia, encouraging cooperation in order to achieve "an effective use of educational resources, an equitable distribution of education services, and the development of innovative concepts and applications" (*Education Cooperation Act,* 1972).

Illinois is in the vanguard in other ways in directing influence toward cooperation. *Phase III of the Master Plan* for higher education in that state speaks about possible "common market" activities: "Possibilities for cooperative programs among the public and private colleges and universities include the broad utilization of high-cost educational resources, such as computers, libraries, and graduate programs, the sharing and interchange ability of special institutional capabilities, such as faculty, programs, and facilities to provide wider educational or community services to the region" (Criteria, 1972). The *Master Plan* also calls for alternative delivery systems, such as nontraditional forms of postsecondary education.

The Education Cooperation Act is designed to implement the intentions of the *Master Plan.* At this writing it is too early to determine what impact the Act will have on interinstitutional cooperation in Illinois. It seems reasonable to assume, however, that this legislation will have considerable effect in that state and will be watched by legislators and coordinating boards in other states. It is likely to be influential in Illinois, however, because specific financial incentives—and guidelines—are offered. Title III provides financial encouragement to consortia, but that legislation as implemented has not related financial incentives to guidelines for improving the effectiveness of cooperation in the same degree that the Illinois legislation does. For most of its history, the consortium movement has depended upon admonition, exhortation, and enlightened self-interest to promote its cause. Concrete fiscal incentives have been wholly lacking at the state level.

But at the federal level, new leverage for educational development and change in higher education may come through the nascent Fund for the Improvement of Postsecondary Education. With its activity authorized by Congress in 1972 and with an initial appropriation for fiscal 1973 in the amount of ten million dollars, the fund has as its fundamental purpose the encouragement of a wide spectrum of people to think creatively about improving the learning options offered in postsecondary education.

The three broad strategies of the fund lie in encouraging institutional self-renewal, new programs for new clientele, and improvement in the teaching-learning process. Little is said in the scant literature of the fund about interinstitutional cooperation, but what is said asserts a preference for providing innovative monies to programs that have the promise of affecting more than a single institution. The Fund for the Improvement of Postsecondary Education has the possibility of effect well beyond its limited appropriations to the degree that it consciously selects to support innovative programs which contain a maximum multiplier potential. At least in theory, the multiplier potential is greater within a group of institutions than in a single college or university. Consortia have a wide open opportunity to argue the case for this advantage if they make presentations to the fund.

The present situation in terms of leadership of the consortium movement is therefore tantalizing. Until Big Brother may come in the form of governmental coordination, a genuine opportunity exists for the consortium movement to be leveraged into a role of importance well beyond what now exists. That role could benefit individual students and institutions, could conserve and perhaps increase diversity in postsecondary education, and could contribute materially to innovative educational development in response to the revolutionary period in which we now live.

A Hypothetical Model

The factors touched on in the foregoing pages suggest some reasonable possibilities for strengthening the existing pattern of interinstitutional cooperation. They reflect what an enlightened conservatism might do about the consortium movement. But they do not depict what is fully needed: a radical mutation in interinstitutional cooperation which would help protect the diversity of higher education, enrich the educational options available to students, enable an intelligent allocation of resources to institutional needs, and temper the encroachment of government on educational decision-making and operations. What is exciting about the position of interinstitutional cooperation in the context of existing or imminent changes in higher education is that such a mutation is possible.

As a crude hypothetical example, imagine a middle-sized American city called Linton, with a characteristic suburban-exurban surround, having three well-known private institutions, a public community college, and a rather select private junior college two to three miles apart within the city limits, a growing state college on the edge of the city, two private institutions in the suburban-exurban fringe, and four major high-technology electronic plants within the total urban perimeter.

One of the private institutions inside the city is Linton University, with six thousand students, including two thousand in graduate study, with nationally respected programs in the arts, sciences, and technology. Of the other two private institutions in Linton, one is Wollstonecraft, a well-established women's college with eighteen hundred students, principally undergraduate, with university-level quality in most of the arts and sciences. The other is St. Gregory College, a Jesuit institution of twenty-eight hundred students, best known to the lay public for its success in intercollegiate football, but with significant academic strengths, undergraduate and graduate, in the humanities.

Linton Community College has an enrollment of thirty-five hundred students, almost wholly local, in contrast to the private university and two colleges, which draw nearly 60 percent of their students from outside the state. Its enrollment is more or less evenly divided into terminal-degree students training for subprofessional occupations and transfer students preparing to go on in the arts and sciences at senior institutions. The private junior college, Fairhurst, enrolls seven hundred young women principally from affluent families and from many parts of the country; some plan to go on to senior colleges, but most conclude their formal education with the program at this junior college, which is well regarded for its education in the fine and performing arts and in the humanities.

Parkes State College, once a normal school engaged solely in the training of elementary school teachers, has grown to an enrollment of nearly four thousand students, some six hundred of whom are in graduate study, mostly in elementary education. The

Parkes State graduate program does not include doctoral-level work. At the undergraduate level, it has become, at least in form, a liberal arts college.

The only PH.D. programs in these institutions are at the private university, except for small doctoral programs in social work at the women's college and in the classics and Romance languages at the Jesuit institution.

One of the private institutions beyond the city is Fulmer, a denominational Protestant undergraduate college of five hundred fifty students. This institution has a long history, but its church-supported status has provided it with only meager academic resources, and it now lives in a precarious financial state. The other private institution out of the city is the Linton Institute of Technology, a four-year institution of good reputation, with eleven hundred students, predominantly male, engaged in undergraduate engineering and other technical studies.

The four major industrial plants in the area employ nearly fifty-eight thousand men and women. The oldest plant, the largest employer of subprofessional labor, manufactures electrical home appliances, with one new division developing in the production of audio cassette recorders and portable video equipment. The other three plants are of more recent vintage and are highly specialized producers of sophisticated electronic components for computers, control systems, and communications. These three industrial centers employ a high proportion of engineers, technologists, and other professionals.

The Linton area is the major financial and banking center for a three-state area. Its attractions include the library of a former president of the United States, a park system (running from the city into three suburbs) which was designed by Frederick Law Olmsted in the nineteenth century, a small but excellent museum of art with particular strength in twentieth-century American painting and graphics, a city public library heavily supported for four generations by the family of the founder of the major electrical industry, a lively "little theater" movement, a modest but good civic symphony orchestra, and a pioneering public television and radio station.

As American urban areas go, the demography of the Linton area has been fairly stable since the end of heavy European immi-

gration in the early 1920s. The bulk of the families of whatever ex-
traction have resided in the city for fifty years, some having had
residence since the first settlement in the 1840s. Ethnic minorities of
Irish and Italian ancestry have increasingly been assimilated into
the population with less and less visibility. Newcomers, attracted by
the colleges and the university and by the electronic industries, have
blended into a mix that is predominantly lower-middle to upper-
middle class and are for the most part white. In the years since
World War II, a small, stable, relatively integrated black population has been augmented by black migration from the northern edge
of the rural South, three states away. These newcomers have settled
principally in one impoverished suburb of Linton, not in the inner
city; the black population of the whole area is 18 percent of the
total population of the area, and 85 percent live in this single suburb.

Approximately one-third of the families of the Linton area
are affiliated with the Roman Catholic Church; another third or
more are relatively active Protestants. Six percent of the total population is Jewish; most of them live in the inner city and one suburb.

The Linton area is thirty-two miles across and is roughly a
single county with some open country. In 1968 the voters approved
by referendum the unification of city and county government into
one Linton Metro District, aimed at consolidating, standardizing,
and improving the support and management of public services.

Education is clearly a significant resource of the area and
has been husbanded and developed in various important ways. Not
the least of these has been the continuing work for the general good
and the financial support provided by five rich families of the area
—two from the financial community (early settlers), the electrical
appliance industry magnate, and two highly successful scientist-in-
ventors whose entrepreneurship created two of the electronic corporations outside the city. Financially, all the institutions of higher
education have problems. Linton University and Wollstonecraft
College are in the best shape; each draws students nationally; their
endowments are $115 million and $54 million respectively. Budgets
at both places are more heavily under control than they were five
years ago but are in delicate balance. Linton University graduate
and research components have been hard hit by retrenchment in
federal science support; tuition and fees at both places verge toward

five thousand dollars a year and even so do not cover real operating costs. The Jesuit college has an endowment of thirty-two million dollars and benefits from a strong interest in admission by the off-spring of prosperous and upward-mobile Catholic families. Even so, these three institutions are feeling the severe pressure of costs on income, and all three have had to borrow from endowment to meet their requirements in the past five years.

The community college had no trouble in its first ten years, but failure of its capital bond measure in 1971 and the unionization of its faculty in 1972 present a new picture. Fairhurst, the private junior college, with little endowment and an expensive plant, has encountered sharply diminished applications each year since 1969 and had a budget deficit in fiscal 1972, repeated and worsened in fiscal 1973. In 1972 the Board of Higher Education ordered Parkes State College to discontinue plans for graduate development, and the state legislature denied it further teaching positions in spite of a 5 percent increase in enrollment. Unionization of the faculty at the state college now appears certain. Fulmer, the exurban Protes-tant denominational college, operating with great parsimony and annual support from the Synod, is managing to keep its head above water, but barely. Admission applications have dropped 5 percent every year since 1970, and the college is now admitting nearly everyone who applies. The Linton Institute of Technology is com-petently managed, but it too has been hit by federal science funds retrenchment, by rising costs, and by uncertainty about the eco-nomic position of technological industries with the phasing out of the space program, the winding down of war-related production, and the like. Applications for admission are down at the institute by 20 percent compared with 1968.

In this context, the presidents of the several colleges and the university are invited by the head of the largest of the new elec-tronic industries—who is also chairman of the trustees of the univer-sity—to meet and discuss what they might do to help their own in-stitutions and each other. After five sessions and outside studies, the Linton Consortium (TLC) is born.

The plan for the new consortium of eight diverse institu-tions is based on seven principles to which the group has committed itself. On them, the group aims to build an interactive complex of postsecondary educational resources whose key elements are the individual colleges and universities themselves, but in which the whole is much greater than the sum of its parts. The groups foresee the new complex helping traditional functions to be performed with increased effectiveness and new projects to be undertaken.

They see themselves in a sense as the founders of a new kind of institution, what some of them speak of as "the University of Linton." This appellation, while it reflects some of the enthusiasm of the founders, is not thought suitable because of the already existing name of Linton University and because not all eight institutions can pretend to offer a university level of education.

At length the group decides to name their invention The Linton Consortium, even though, as one heavy-humored academic wag points out, the initial letters of the title, TLC, might be confused by some with the popular shorthand for "tender loving care." More seriously, the group likes the nonspecific TLC title because it wants the new complex to interact with other constituencies and resources of the area: the industries, the museum, the presidential library, the public broadcasting station, and others.

In any case, the seven principles articulated are the following:

(1) That the new consortium should improve the quality and range of education available to students in each of its constituent institutions.

(2) That, within the consortium, each institution should preserve its identity and maintain as much autonomy as the constraints of serious cooperation permit.

(3) That the consortium should minimize duplication of education programs and redundancy of facilities and should aim at complementarity of academic programs and facilities among its constituent institutions.

(4) That the consortium should seek to reduce or control institutional operating costs by collective means wherever possible.

(5) That the consortium should give central assistance in financial development to member institutions and have a fund-raising capacity for collective needs.

(6) That the consortium should provide planning, development, and coordination for new collective educational programs responsive to changing needs and new clientele in the area.

(7) That the governance and executive part of the consortium should have authority equivalent to its responsibility for leadership.

The governance and administration part of the new consortium is designed to assume final responsibility and authority for the group in these fields, as well as in long-range planning, provision of specialized services, and development of new models of educational service delivery.

The group agrees upon a governing structure that places policy authority and responsibility in the hands of twenty-five members of a consortium board of trustees. The members are the eight institutional board chairmen or their trustee-surrogates, the eight institutional presidents, eight public members elected by the others, and the chancellor of the consortium. Provision is made for a chairman, vice-chairman, and secretary to be elected by the board, and four standing committees are established: the Executive Committee, the Committee on Educational Policy, the Committee on Administration and Finance, and the Committee on Planning and Development. The Executive Committee is chaired by the board chairman, with the eight presidents plus the chancellor as members; the three other committees have a lay trustee chairman plus three lay trustees and three presidential trustees. The chancellor and board chairman are members of all standing and temporary committees in addition to the Executive Committee. The board will meet regularly four times a year; the Executive Committee will meet monthly; and other standing committees will meet regularly well in advance of board sessions.

For important advisory assistance in its consideration and development of policy, the board has the help of two bodies—the Academic Council and the Consortium Council. The Academic Council provides consortium faculty and students with a medium for discussing policy development and for advising the board. Its forty-eight members are four faculty members and two students elected annually from each of the eight institutions. It meets semiannually in the fall and spring and is chaired by the chancellor, through whom its agenda is formulated. The Consortium Council is a formal advisory group of leading men and women of the Linton area not otherwise related to the cooperating institutions as profes-

sionals, students, or trustees. This select group of thirty-two citizens
includes representatives from the nonconsortium cultural resources
of the area, from the Linton financial district, from the federal and
state legislators elected by the district, from minority groups, and
others. The Consortium Council also meets semiannually in the fall
and spring at the call of the chairman of the consortium.

The chancellor is first among equals with the eight institutional presidents. This position is considered essential by the planning group because of their understanding of the disadvantages of
weak executive leadership, their belief that due authority should
accompany assigned responsibility, and their conclusion that the
central consortium structure should have significant coordinating
strength in specified areas of cooperation.

Three other senior executive positions are established. One
is that of academic vice-chancellor, who provides staff support to
the board Committee on Educational Policy, administers consortium
cooperative educational programs, works closely with senior academic officers and faculty of the participating institutions, and assists the Academic Council. A second position is that of vice-chancellor for administration and finance, who gives staff support to the
board Committee on Administration and Finance, administers the
central business and service operations of the consortium, provides
liaison with federal and state governments, works closely with the
senior business and administrative officers of the cooperating institutions, and maintains active relationships with industry in the area.
The third position is that of vice-chancellor for planning and development, who has responsibility for ongoing policy planning and
consortium development, including principal staff support to the
board Committee on Planning and Development, staff research and
evaluation related to new policies and plans, close work with other
academic and administrative officers concerned with planning at
the consortium level and in the cooperating institutions, and preparation of consortium fund-raising proposals for grants and gifts.

The planning group concludes that TLC requires a minimum
operating budget for its staff of two hundred fifty thousand dollars
a year, and this sum has to be guaranteed by a two-part fee structure for member institutions: seventy-five hundred dollars from

each institution annually, plus a contribution of ten dollars for each full-time student. This basic commitment assures the consortium of a small permanent staff and operating capability. Program support beyond this amount must come from outside public and private sources through consortium fund-raising. Special service activities, such as an international study program, depend, as in most consortia, on special fees.

TLC suggests some of the essential features that interinstitutional cooperation must have in its charter assumptions and organizational structure if it is to provide for a radical improvement in collective operations. These essential features revolve around certain basic decisions: to agree to principles that give to the consortium some of the action reserved before to the individual institutions; to agree to a collective policy-making structure with superordinate power in these spheres of action; to agree to an operating organization for the consortium whose executive is, in relation to the institutional presidents, first among equals. Decisions of this kind are necessary but not sufficient conditions for the establishment of a really effective consortium of colleges and universities. Their absence or incompleteness in nearly all present consortia account for much of the difficulty the movement has had in achieving an optimum cooperative rationalization of academic and economic operations or in innovating substantially in new models of postsecondary education. One of the most important additional conditions needed, and almost wholly absent now in the consortium scene, is a commitment and structure of personnel involvement that will encourage faculty members and others to find some significant part of their security and reward in interinstitutional service.

Sidney Tickton, in a private communication to me, has urged this fundamental need. In his view, the need could be supplied by using budget as an effective management tool, rather than simply a cost-cutting device. According to Tickton, the budget-making process can offer (1) savings through better management which can be shared with other educational efforts or used to provide greater or better educational services; (2) recognition of the duplication of programs at various institutions; (3) identification of the possibilities of sharing facilities between institutions that are overcrowded and those that have surplus space; (4) money, prestige, and power behind new ideas for combined action; and (5) tangible incentives in the form of funds for cooperative activity.

TLC therefore needs to look toward ways that institutional budgets can be constructed and controlled within a consortium framework, to find ways to discourage redundancy and waste and to establish incentives for cooperative activities by faculty and others. This turns out to be the most difficult effort undertaken by TLC.

Through the Committee on Administration and Finance and the consortium board, TLC is first granted authority by its constituent member institutions (including the two public colleges, by permission of the state legislature) to have a quarterly review of institutional budget preparation and final approval over the annual budgets proposed within the consortium. Second, TLC establishes a central fund, called the Linton Foundation, to give selective support to TLC faculty undertaking the development of new cooperative programs or contributing to existing cooperation.

The foundation is begun with two principal sources of funds, both of which can have continuity: the corporate foundations of the three major electronics firms and the budgets of the constituent institutions. The combined foundations of the industrial firms agree to contribute up to three hundred forty thousand dollars to the foundation annually for five years, providing this sum is matched by the TLC member institutions, each contributing at an equal rate (approximately 0.5 percent) of its operating budget during the same period. With nearly seven hundred thousand dollars a year from these sources and the possibility of grant funds from public sources and national foundations, the Linton Foundation can give incentive grants to individual faculty and faculty groups. Through faculty salary supplements and other means, Linton Foundation money exercises leverage toward cooperation. The fact that TLC has significant funding available for programmatic development gives it a credibility among institutional faculty members which few ordinary consortia gain. Faculty members now see themselves as part of the consortium, through which they can acquire direct advantages. Each institution also establishes, as part of its regular continuing budget, one faculty position wholly devoted to TLC academic programing, utilizable throughout the consortium. This step attracts a large outside foundation to the extent that it agrees to fund eight more such TLC professorships for a five-year period, renewable for a second five years.

Diverse as the eight colleges and universities are, a number of financial, economic, and business operations activities can be consolidated and rationalized. In the first year, TLC accomplishes two fundamental intensive studies, with expert, independent outside assistance, under the Committee on Administration and Finance. One of these is of the economic status of each member institution, its resources, needs, and performance, plus a projection of alternative models for collective economic interaction available to the consortium. The institutional status evaluations are valuable both to the individual colleges and the university (in certain cases carrying an ice-water shock effect) and to TLC in determining the most promising basic policies and guidelines needed to strengthen collective financial and business operations. The second study reviews existing management practices at the institutional level and recommends standardizing and coordinating management procedures and services within the consortium.

After thorough discussion in the policy bodies of the institutions and TLC, these studies have numerous results. A continuing periodic economic review is established, using the first study as a base; a continuing pattern of long-range economic projection and planning is set, with the Committee on Planning and Development playing a principal part. Coordinated decision-making about the allocation of resources and the development of institutional strengths and the consequent consolidation of functions and services leads to a joint admissions and student recruitment program, pooled purchasing, centralization of major computer installations and services at the university, pooled insurance programs, standardization of accounting procedures and business record-keeping, a cooperative student financial aid service, an intercampus bus system, among many other projects. Most important, the studies result in actions to coordinate the planning not only of institutional operating budgets, but also of major capital outlay projects in order to avoid redundancy.

Another benefit of undergirding organizational commitments

and budget leverage is their contribution to the development of academic complementarity and cooperation. An intensive year-long academic planning effort under the Committee on Educational Policy, with participation by representatives of the Academic Council, leads to a series of recommendations which are approved by the consortium board and accepted by the eight institutions. These actions include substantial coordination of institutional calendars and schedules, student interchange course enrollment arrangements, decisions about differential educational missions for the several campuses, control at TLC over the approval of new educational programs in order to avoid wasteful duplication, joint faculty appointments, conversion of all TLC library cataloguing to the Library of Congress system, establishment of a TLC union catalogue, coordination of the further development of library holdings, establishment of a system for expeditious interlibrary lending within TLC, concentration of further development of graduate education at the university, and intercampus contracting for academic service and space.

In the realm of collective development of new modes and alternatives in postsecondary education, TLC early begins to realize some exciting possibilities. The razing of the walls of institutional separatism and the pooling of ideas, academic expertise, and financial resources brings Linton higher education into a new dynamic relationship with other resources and needs of the area. By combining the diversity of its institutions within the unity of a strong consortium, TLC is able to establish a video system connecting its institutions and the major electronics firms and banks of the area, permitting not only intercampus video course offerings but a paid-fee offering of courses to personnel located at their worksites; to connect this TLC system with the Linton cablevision community network and the independent public television station, making it possible for TLC faculty and students to engage in creative, educational, and civic programing valuable to the whole area; to use both of these interacting systems to enlarge the availability of college-level instruction to all residents of the Linton area regardless of age; to help open access to college experience to high school students in significant ways in addition to the usual graduation route, both by enabling students, if ready, to move into college work prior to graduation, and by providing a consortium Second-Chance Center for educationally disadvantaged nongraduates. Many other innovative possibilities come to pass in TLC as it rationalizes collective planning, economic operations, and academic programing, and brings together a cooperative decision-making group with resources far beyond those of any single campus in the group.

Thus, highly oversimplified, we have in TLC a model of what can be done. Whether it will happen, as Becky Sharp might have said, *depends.*

As it awaits leadership that may move it toward planned academic complementarity, joint planning in capital outlay, and innovative entrepreneurship, interinstitutional cooperation remains at present an empty shibboleth for the most part. Cooperation is necessary, but the dead hand of the past, in terms of the strong tradition of institutional autonomy, impedes effective cooperative action and tends to foreclose cooperative leadership from within institutions.

Events and pressures that face higher education in the foreseeable future will make institutional autonomy less and less tenable as the norm. Cooperation and coordination are essential and will come, intelligently and wisely or not. The need for educational leadership to go beyond the present nature of the consortium movement to genuine collaboration on problems and possibilities is attested to enough. But for this to happen, there will have to be some surrendering of autonomy, some better identification of common problems, and some greater willingness by government and foundation to provide incentives and rewards for cooperation. Getting these three things will not be at all easy.

It is likely in the short-term future that tensions between the public and private sectors will increase, that competition among the various segments of public education will increase, and that private institutions will join with each other more to oppose the public sector than to engage in constructive cooperation of an academic kind. But beyond this period of tension, the impulse toward greater rationalization of public and private resources for higher education will survive. So too will the need for more imaginative innovation and development in response to changes in the society and its expectations of education.

The only real hope that institutional autonomy might be broken lies in the function of financial pressure. On the negative side, institutional autonomy may give way to the requirements of cooperation or coordination if the situation of colleges and universities in the older institutional model becomes desperate enough in the scramble for students and financial resources. On the positive side, institutional autonomy may give way to cooperation if external agencies such as state legislatures, coordinating bodies, and private foundations can conceive and offer financial incentives that will cause educational leadership to move toward interinstitutional innovation and development.

Part of the nature of the revolutionary period in which American higher education exists is that the old institutional model of the college and university is obsolete and doesn't yet know it. Students know it, and are demonstrating their awareness by shifting from institution to institution, by "stopping out," by shopping in the educational marketplace, and by helping in the invention of alternative modes of postsecondary education. Many government officials, including state legislators, governors, and people in the federal government, are recognizing the need for change and development in higher education. The same is true of special study commissions, of many foundation executives, and others interested in the effectiveness of education in our society. But the behavior of trustees, administrators, and faculties in the colleges and universities does not exhibit a similar awareness.

Richard Millard, director of Higher Education Services of the Education Commission of the States, has stated that the best promise lies in effective interaction between voluntary cooperative groups of institutions and state coordinating boards (1972). At best, this would be a most happy marriage of voluntary and directive factors. Given the kind of action the state of Illinois is taking, it is certainly possible to imagine a healthy development of voluntary consortia in that state working in harmony with the Board of Higher Education. The Illinois example is instructive, however. To move voluntary cooperation beyond the limits that institutional autonomy would put upon it, to come to a bolder vision and actuality, requires a kind of intervention that individual institutions themselves apparently cannot supply.

Chapter 7

WHAT TO DO UNTIL BIG BROTHER COMES

The preceding chapter outlined some of the possibilities for consortia in the future. Most of these possibilities clearly hinge on some very big *ifs*. This concluding chapter summarizes my main findings and presents recommendations that could increase the possibilities of consortia becoming a significant factor in American higher education. But without some attention and intervention from elected officials and officers in foundations and government, the consortium movement is not likely to serve higher education and our society adequately. There can be little hope in expecting consortia to be better than they are as the result of college presidents, unassisted, suddenly seeing a great light on the road to Damascus. Presidents are too preoccupied with other commitments, including day-to-day institutional survival. And, like their institutions, they are not really prepared to give up any sovereignty on their own.

Some General Findings

On the positive side, one cannot help but be impressed, as I have been in visiting consortia, with their collective track record.

There is no doubt that the main conclusion of a 1972 study by the Management Division of the Academy for Educational Development (AED) has a certain validity: "Significant cooperation among colleges and universities, the subject of more talk than action in the past, is on the upswing. Whether on their own initiative or by legislative mandate, more and more institutions of higher education are working together on problems they can no longer solve alone" (Schwenkmeyer and Goodman, 1972, p. 1).

One can inventory, as AED did, an impressively long list of activities in which consortia are now engaged: In administrative and business services, joint business operations, training to improve management, collective public-private purchasing, free or carefully-costed interinstitutional enrollment, joint computer facilities, telephone networking, fuel oil savings, and lower insurance rates. In enrollment and admissions, such activities as the Single Application Method of the Associated Colleges of the Midwest, joint student recruitment of the United Independent Colleges of Art and other cooperative approaches to the student market. In academic programs, the combined field of study approach developed by the Worcester Consortium for Higher Education, joint programs in the New Orleans Consortium, a few collective decisions to phase out redundant graduate and undergraduate offerings, consortium-enlarged choices of courses for concentration, TAGER's use of television, jointly sponsored field study opportunities, and some fifteen other examples of cooperation. And in library operations, student services, community services, and faculty utilization and development additional constructive contributions.

At the same time, a careful examination makes it clear that the inventory is still a thin one. The AED list like my own case examinations, confirms the candid observation that for the most part, "consortia cooperate on the easy things." Further, examples drawn from the movement as a whole, as is the AED inventory, can give a distorted sense of the scope of individual consortia. Taken one by one, consortia have things to be proud of, but few if any exemplify the kind of across-the-board development that a casual reading of the AED examples may suggest. Things just are not that good.

Rather than simply listing as many current cooperative activities as possible and implying that these only need multiplication for the consortium movement to reach full flower, it is necessary to extract from the data analytic conclusions that point towards possible action of real consequence. The five major conclusions I have come to about the consortium movement in American higher education can be put briefly:

First, the need for maximum effective voluntary cooperation by groups of colleges and universities is critical. This is hardly news. I will not rehearse the fiscal, academic, social, and other reasons why the need for strong cooperation is so critical. The issues of institutional survival, quality, adequate educational service, societal allocation of resources for education, and all the rest are well enough known, at least abstractly, to anyone likely to read this book. What is really worrisome about this need, however, is that, while most presidents—and even some faculty and trustees—can verbalize it, our colleges and universities are not yet acting as though they understood it.

Second, the consortium movement is not adequately meeting this need. Despite all the constructive achievements of consortia and the valiant efforts of the majority of consortia directors to do a great deal with too little of everything, the consortium movement fails as yet to meet the critical need that exists for effective interinstitutional cooperation. Consortia generally have so far not succeeded in achieving planned academic complementarity and substantial academic cooperation; they have not touched the edge of cooperative, complementary capital outlay planning among their institutions; they have only just begun to rationalize business and administrative operations on a joint basis; and they have not been a major source of innovation in the delivery of educational services to existing or possible new clienteles. Some consortia stand out in trying to meet the need for cooperation; most make an effort within serious limits; and some seem like paper organizations. None comes up to the need adequately.

Third, the principal direct impediment to effective interinstitutional cooperation is the traditional commitment of colleges and universities to institutional autonomy. The lag between what consortia are and what they ought to be cannot be laid to the professional staffs of cooperative groups. The fault lies not in their staffs but in their institutional leaders and faculties. Even when two universities merge into one corporate identity, the old pattern of institutional autonomy dies hard. In most consortia, it does not really die at all. Voluntary euthanasia is hardly a popular custom anywhere in the human enterprise; it is, and seems likely to remain, a solution unexplored by institutional sovereignty. Presidents are apt to be fluent in the rhetoric of cooperation and even comfortable about its reality as long as cooperation is about "easy things." But when an executive director pushes too close to the hard things that may mean giving up some significant separate institutional ambitions or commitments, his days with the consortium usually are numbered.

Fourth, institutional autonomy should be modified, not killed; and for most institutions, voluntary cooperation may be the only means by which it can survive at all. In an increasingly homogenized and standardized mass society, the relative autonomy and decentralization of educational institutions would be a costly thing to lose. The great value of independence for colleges and universities and for new vehicles of postsecondary education consists in the protection it provides for education against uniformity and control imposed by influences more concerned with other priorities than those of learning and teaching.

We are at the end of an era in which such independence could be guaranteed by institutional separatism. Economic reality and forces of social change are making the older institutional model itself unfeasible. Change may go in the direction of liquidating the least feasible institutions and imposing coordination on the others. This is already happening in the public sector with the appearance of state superboards, the consolidation of institutions, and the removal of significant elements of planning and decision-making from institutional hands. The possibility exists in Section 1202 of the Higher Education Act of 1965 as altered by the Education Amendments of 1972, that federal initiative will accelerate this development (Circular Letter No. 19, 1972). As private institutions come to receive more public funds, they are more and more likely to be drawn into systems of coordination and control, with erosion of their autonomy.

Both public and private institutions could find some protection for their basic institutional freedom by voluntarily giving some of it up in consortia that provide collective strength educationally and politically as well as mechanisms for achieving more efficient use of available economic resources. Strong consortia could work well with strong state coordinating boards, with advantages both to individual institutions and to the public interest.

Fifth, the achievement of an adequately effective consortium movement will depend on intelligent outside intervention and support. What we have in the present consortium movement are very modest attainments sufficient to attest to the nature of the need they are beginning to serve. We have the beginnings of the kind of knowledgeable, competent professional staff an adequate consortium movement would require. And we have many presidents and others who may be at a point where, *given impetus,* they would be ready to move beyond words and "easy things." But we have also the dead hand of the past.

I find myself less than patient with the view that, since voluntary consortia have failed to do anything very basic, they therefore do not merit government or foundation support of more than an incidental or casual kind. It is understandable that some college and university presidents privately deprecate the very consortia to which their institutions belong: What is deprecated clearly is nothing unto which to render up any sovereignty. But it is harder to understand why foundation and government officers do not see that if real interinstitutional cooperation is needed, and voluntary consortia are not yet adequately meeting the need, the *only* road to go in the matter is to find ways to make consortia more effective. Basically, this means providing money that will cause institutions, in their own short-run interest, to give up some autonomy, identify fundamental common problems, and get to work on them.

For major continuing support incentives, intervention can come only from government. On the federal side, Title III has made an important start, but only that. It would be inexcusable for the Office of Education to maintain Title III funding in the future principally as a way of giving individual institutions help under a "cooperative" umbrella. The Title III legislation and guidelines should be recast to induce the kind of deeper cooperation that is needed. On the state side, all governors and legislators should take note of Illinois' cooperation-support program reported in the preceding chapter.

For the support of ancillary national services like those provided through the consortium center of the American Association for Higher Education, for planning that has promise of leading to qualitative breakthroughs, and for potentially significant innovation, responsibility lies mainly with the foundations. These activities simply and regrettably will not be supported enough by the very institutions that can benefit from them, but it is not responsible for the foundations to turn their backs on consortia as a result. Because colleges and universities will not do enough on their own, it is necessary for agencies not hamstrung by the baggage of institutional autonomy to provide leadership. The consortium movement goes at a pedestrian pace. Money wisely invested by foundations could improve that pace.

The Godfather Strategy

The five conclusions summarized above suggest a strategy for the development of stronger consortia in American higher education. The logic of the strategy is simple, but accomplishing it will be difficult.

Time is not an ally in its accomplishment. The conditions under which colleges and universities operate today are changing rapidly, perhaps more rapidly than higher education leadership fully understands. As a consequence, there is no abundance of time in which the voluntary cooperation movement can slowly mature. Many private colleges and universities are already insecure: Retrenchment, severe budgetary measures, faculty cutbacks, and other signs of deep crisis are the order of the day. Public colleges and universities, too, face swift change, with all of them encountering new budget constraints and new measures of control from higher public authority. If voluntary cooperation is to help the viability of colleges and universities soon enough, and if institutional autonomy is not to lose major ground to Big Brother, something better than muddling through is going to have to happen.

The strategy I suggest for "something better" depends principally on bold intervention in the consortium movement by foundations and by officials and agencies of government. Up to now, foundations and government for the most part have settled for too little with the consortium movement. Not only have they been parsimonious in responding to consortium requests for help, they have not often used their funds to induce consortia to move on the "hard things" of cooperation. It is time they did. It is not enough for great foundation undertakings like the Carnegie Commission on Higher Education simply to say that interinstitutional cooperation is very desirable and leave the matter at that. No amount of sunny statements about cooperation, no viewing with alarm, no cynicism about the slight accomplishments of consortia, and certainly no plethora of preaching at institutional presidents will do the job. What is needed is some substantial, positive action by those outside the consortium movement with enough resources to cause it to turn around. To get institutional leaders to modify institutional autonomy and build stronger consortia will take what the Godfather knew would always work: "an offer they can't refuse."

Lest my facetious reference to the Godfather in describing a strategy of intervention should repel government and foundation officers who have little desire to be cast as a kind of educational Mafia, let me put it another way. I am suggesting only that, in face of a serious need of our society and in the absence of other effective leadership, they should deliberately use some of the resources they command as incentives to lead and encourage the consortium movement to higher ground.

In Chapter Six, I mentioned Sidney Tickton's description of financial incentives for participation in cooperative activities as the "green carrot." It is absolutely essential that federal and state governments be geared to provide such motivation for the *development* of cooperation, not simply for the maintenance of its shadow. Further federal support for cooperative groups under Title III must be made fundamentally contingent upon demonstrated intention and performance of institutions to work together. And state governments must recognize their responsibility to make institutional support contingent upon cooperation of a solid, demonstrated kind.

Two additional steps are imperative for government and foundations. The first is to provide a strong incentive for faculty involvement in cooperative programs. Alden Dunham is correct in saying that "unless there is strong incentive for faculty involvement, a consortium will fail, certainly as far as academic complementarity is concerned" (1973). It would be entirely practical for federal and state guidelines to stress faculty involvement by funding inter-institutional joint appointments, supplementing faculty salaries for cooperative undertakings, supporting faculty development of interinstitutional curriculum programs, and the like.

The other step that needs to be taken is to increase the budgetary leverage of the consortium organization itself. Guidelines for federal and state funding, unlike the present Title III, should provide resources and resource control to consortia directly. In this connection, Robert H. McCambridge, Assistant Commissioner for Higher Education Planning in New York, has written (1973):

> There is an important relationship between some of the problems of the voluntary consortium and the need for a power base through either the delegation of power by institutions to a central body, which I think is not likely to come, or power as the result of the availability of money to support worthy causes and objectives. . . . If there is to be any significant change in, let us say, educational offerings, or vigorous coordination in terms of encouraging or restricting institutional initiatives, there must be positive or negative incentives that can be used by the interinstitutional body with assurance of power to act. The consortial movement has been based upon voluntarism where everyone and anyone can exercise a veto. It is obvious that this does not constitute a strong base for significant change.

In a word, money must be made available to consortia on the condition that they centralize significant decision-making power and thereby demonstrate a capability to get things done. Such funding would mean that, beyond institutional contributions, the consortium corporate entity would have a fiscal credibility and strength it seldom has at present.

There are many specific ways in which government and foundations can do this within the bounds of good sense and intelligent social responsibility:

First, a major national conference or commission on new directions in interinstitutional cooperation. There is an urgent need for high-level consideration of the consortium movement, the establishment of clear goals for modifying institutional autonomy in the direction of effective cooperation, the specification of means for achieving these goals, and, in particular, the redefinition of the federal role *vis-à-vis* consortia. Until now, the national conferences that have been held in the consortium movement have not been at this level of influence. Meetings of consortium executives simply cannot have the visibility, reach, or impact that is needed.

The Carnegie Commission on Higher Education has come to the end of its work. In all of its studies, it has only touched on the consortium movement, even though it strongly endorses inter-institutional cooperation. Many of its recommendations are of potentially profound importance to American society. But to be realized that potential must have follow-through beyond the Commission, such as national attention to the future of voluntary consortia. The national conference or commission on new directions in inter-institutional cooperation could be established either directly by a foundation such as the Carnegie Corporation or through an existing organization such as the American Council on Education or the American Association for Higher Education. Whatever the route, it should be comprised of national leaders from public life as well as from higher education, and should have a deadline of no more than one year in which to produce its work.

This conference or commission should establish as clearly and concretely as possible the agenda of cooperation to which institutions and consortia in the country should attend in the rest of this decade. An equally important job would be to propose new amendments to Title III of the Higher Education Act of 1965 which would provide stronger incentives for substantive cooperation among institutions, and apprise the public and the Congress of its findings.

Second, a legislative study commission of the states to clarify and make more effective the role of state government in encouraging voluntary cooperation among public and private institutions. State governments, as noted earlier, are increasingly engaged with the coordination of higher education and with difficult budgetary concerns stemming from the needs and aspirations of both public and private colleges and universities. Through the work of Richard Millard, Director of Higher Education Services of the Education Commission of the States, and others, state officials are beginning to consider interaction between state coordinating agencies and voluntary consortia and to use state support to encourage interinstitutional cooperation. But much more needs to be done.

One of the most prominent needs is to increase the understanding of state legislative and executive leaders with regard to the potentialities and needs of voluntary consortia. Another is to provide them with information and guidance for developing legislation to promote interinstitutional cooperation. To serve both needs, a one-year legislative study commission should be organized in cooperation with the Education Commission of the States and the National Legislative Leaders Conference. (The latter group includes all of the top officers of all of the legislatures of the fifty states.) A principal goal of the commission would be to draft model legislation on interinstitutional cooperation. Neither the Education Commission of the States nor the National Legislative Leaders Conference currently has resources with which to underwrite such a commission; but both would be likely to respond favorably to the opportunity if it were funded by other sources such as a foundation.

Third, establishment for five years of an independent private funding agency to seek and selectively support proposals for long-range consortium planning, the development of innovations in cooperation, and the initial demonstration of substantive new programs of cooperation. It is impractical for private foundations or public ones like the Fund for the Improvement of Postsecondary Education to be relied upon for operating support of consortia. Consortium budget requirements can realistically be met only by a combination of institutional assessments, state support, and federal funds. But there is a critical need for support of experimental new departures in the consortium field, and it is reasonable and right to expect this kind of support from foundations.

At present the position of consortia relative to securing foundation grants for experimentation and innovation is very poor. No foundation has placed interinstitutional cooperation in a high category within its own program. No foundation has set up a grant program which would specifically provide incentives to voluntary consortia to break new ground in modifying institutional autonomy and creating substantive cooperation in academic areas, business operations, and capital outlay. In the present situation, therefore, foundations are exercising very little leverage that would help develop and improve interinstitutional cooperation. Relatively small amounts of money, compared to the many millions of dollars that consortia are budgeting in their current operations, could have considerable effect on the future course of consortium development.

At present, consortium proposals for foundation support are not characteristically focused on substantial change or presented to recognizably interested sources of support. Undisciplined by selective change-oriented criteria, they are made on a catch-as-catch-can basis to any foundation where there seems to be a chance of support. The net result is not very productive either for consortia, for foundations, or for the academic or financial improvement of higher education. Serious consideration should therefore be given by one or more foundations to the establishment for a period of five years of a free-standing fund to give selective support to proposals for improving interinstitutional cooperation through relatively small but high-leverage grants. Such a fund would be analogous to the Educational Facilities Laboratory, created some years ago by The Ford Foundation, which has ably demonstrated how an agency with limited resources and a very small staff, addressing itself to one particular aspect of change in education, can be remarkably effective. Its grants have been small, but they have been creatively applied to points of significant change in the evolution of the design, architecture, and use of physical plant in schools and colleges. Something equally successful could be done by a fund creatively devoted to the support of pioneering projects in the improvement of inter-institutional cooperation.

For long-range planning, grants of such a free-standing fund would go to consortia that gave most serious evidence of readiness to provide institutional commitment *and* to modify institutional autonomy in the direction of planned academic complementarity and fiscal cooperation. For innovation and demonstration, the fund would provide grants to consortia where it appeared that support would trigger, not wholly support, the implementation of cooperative innovations of consequence.

Fourth, the establishment of a five-year grant to a center for research and development in higher education to undertake applied research in interinstitutional cooperation and to disseminate its findings in lay language to trustees, presidents, faculties, foundations, and the public. The need for and potential educational value of such applied research is very great. In a few places, as at the Center for Research and Development in Higher Education at Berkeley, the need is beginning to be addressed. The Berkeley studies of the impact of Title III and of consortium economics suggest part of a much bigger job that needs to be done. The base for the applied research that is needed could be provided by an existing center, such as that at Berkeley, or by a new center with access to resources and scholarship.

Support within such a center should be given to continuing and substantial studies of the economics of interinstitutional cooperation, the organization and management of consortia that are moving toward maximum effective cooperation, the critical evaluation of selected consortia, and the evaluation of state programs related to cooperation. For example, it would be useful to evaluate TAGER's operation in depth to see what promise this model of technological/academic cooperation may have for consortia elsewhere, and to assess the status, prospects, and needs of state programs, such as the New York effort on regionalization and the Illinois effort to encourage cooperation through state funding.

Of greatest importance in this applied research is something that is not being done effectively by Berkeley or any other center as yet: the translation of research findings into clear, simple, concise lay language in reports regularly communicated to trustees, presidents, and others who need to know more than they know now in making decisions about cooperation.

Fifth, support of the consortium service center at the American Association for Higher Education for a period of five years. The Cooperative Programs Service, located at AAHE headquarters since the summer of 1972, could, with adequate support, make a number of significant contributions to the task of building more fundamental interinstitutional cooperation in the United States.

AAHE is rightly viewed by the Fund for the Improvement of Postsecondary Education as a promising umbrella for many activities related to innovation and its diffusion in higher education. A properly supported consortium service center within AAHE would be a very useful program objective for the Fund or for private foundations aware of the critical need to help higher education move towards maximum effective cooperation among institutions. Whatever its source of support beyond its current Danforth Foundation grant, this additional funding must be secured soon. The time in which it may be possible to affect the consortium movement, enlarging the substantive effectiveness of voluntary cooperation, is not open-ended.

With only one half-time professional, the AAHE service center is able to do little more than Lewis Patterson was able to accomplish when his informal service center was based at the Kansas City Regional Council for Higher Education. Patterson and AAHE leaders understand the critical need for effective cooperation and what needs to be done for its achievement. With a small full-time staff and little additional funding, the AAHE center could exercise strong influence on the course of the consortium movement. It could serve as an efficient clearinghouse and information base for consortia *and* the leaders of participating colleges and universities. Lewis Patterson is universally regarded in the consortium movement as the person to turn to for such central data as are available; but his clearinghouse function does not presently extend as usefully to decision-makers in colleges and universities as it does to consortia executives and staff. Trustees, presidents, academic deans, legislators, and others should be getting concise, well-written reports on programs and possibilities of cooperation. Economic studies, descriptions and evaluations of cooperative academic innovations, analyses of interaction between state coordinating bodies and voluntary consortia, summaries of long-range consortium planning, and the like, should be going to those institutional and governmental decision-makers on whom the future shape of postsecondary education depends.

The center should also organize and convene state or regional conferences designed to bring state coordinating boards and consortia into productive dialogue with each other. A first step in this direction was a three-day conference at Wingspread in Wisconsin in February 1973, sponsored by the Johnson Foundation at the request of AAHE and the Education Commission of the States. This conference, which brought together approximately forty people more or less equally representative of state coordinating boards and consortia, illustrates what is needed on a continuous basis in all regions of the country.

The service center could also conduct brief intensive summer seminars for teams of presidents and trustees in the practical *why* and *how* of more effective interinstitutional cooperation. No effort is now being made to educate educators about this issue, except for a certain amount of scattered exhortation to which institutional leaders respond with acquiescence as easy as it is nominal. To get busy, preoccupied leaders into a real learning experience takes a special effort, so seminars would have to have built-in incentives for attendance, and be time-limited, expertly conducted, and very practical in orientation.

Finally, the center could provide professional training for consortia staff personnel. The semiannual sessions of the Academic Consortium Seminar, held in conjunction with the annual meetings of the American Council on Education and the AAHE, contribute to the professional development of consortia personnel and should be continued as a self-supporting series. But beyond the seminar, the AAHE service center and related consortia could very usefully provide internships for junior personnel, summer workshops, and other training experiences.

In sum, the problems and prospects of consortia are closely related to the condition of colleges and universities themselves. Consortia, such as they are, are born of the problems of higher education in a time of immense change. Their prospects, positive or negative, depend on what colleges and universities can be induced to do about them. The field of forces in which higher education exists today will inevitably modify the traditional autonomy of most institutions. We will see greater demand for accountability, more press towards rationalization of the academic economy, more mobile free-market behavior by students, more invention of alternative models of postsecondary education, more use of communications technology, and much else.

The outcome may not be happy. If the field of forces does not result in capturing and enlarging what is good and constructive in voluntary cooperation, much of the rich diversity of institutional higher education is likely to be lost in a new standardization imposed by government. If colleges and universities cannot be induced to cooperate effectively, many of them will either be absorbed into a larger apparatus, survive at a level of diminished quality, or not survive at all. The ultimate losers would be the students, denied a range of choices wider and deeper than even now is possible.

The consortium movement may turn out to be only what the apprehensive idealist, Henry Munroe, called it: "a glorious dream." In fact, in 1974, it is not actually very glorious, more often than not turning out to be pretty pedestrian, promising more than it delivers. But it *could* be the threshold of a new era in an American mode of higher education that preserves and enlarges independence, diversity, and quality through intelligent interdependence. This depends almost wholly on what presidents and trustees and faculties do about it. And what *they* do, will depend almost wholly on what wise and forward-looking outsiders in government and philanthropy do, and how soon they act, if at all.

PROFILES OF CONSORTIA

These profiles provide the reader with summary information about nearly ninety consortia of institutions of higher education, including the director, address, and telephone number of each consortium; the member institutions; and a summary of its major activities.

ACADEMIC AFFAIRS CONFERENCE OF MIDWESTERN UNIVERSITIES. Harold E. Walker, Executive Director. Holman Center, Terre Haute, Indiana 47809. 812/232-6311, ext. 2811.

Ball State University, Muncie, Indiana; Illinois State University, Normal; Indiana State University, Terre Haute; Northern Illinois University, DeKalb; Southern Illinois University at Carbondale.

Among AACMU programs and plans are increased number of transferable graduate hours for the master's degree; a Visiting Scholar Program at the doctoral level; development of a cooperative Urban Center in Chicago with dormitory, conference, and office facilities; administrative internships and graduate assistant opportunities for minorities; proposals for technical assistance in education; and cooperative programs with other consortia and educational agencies.

ALABAMA CENTER FOR HIGHER EDUCATION. Richard Arrington, Jr.,

Executive Director. 2121 Eighth Avenue, North, Suite 1011, Birmingham, Alabama 35203.

Alabama A & M University, Huntsville; Alabama State University, Montgomery; Daniel Payne College, Birmingham; Miles College, Birmingham; Oakwood College, Huntsville; Stillman College, Tuscaloosa; Talladega College, Talladega; Tuskegee Institute, Tuskegee Institute, Alabama.

ACHE is developing programs in administrative improvement (one-week sessions for administrative and academic leaders of member institutions); curriculum development (cooperative degree programs in engineering, veterinary medicine, physics, and architecture; cooperative education-planning; and coordination of student teaching); student personnel (a proposed cooperative counseling and recruitment center); library development (the Cooperative College Library Center for joint purchasing and processing, and the Collection and Evaluation of Materials about Black Americans Archives); faculty development (Drug Education Institute, Integrated Humanities Institute, and Media Workshop); Cultural Enrichment (joint bookings of lyceum programs and Negro History Week Festival); inservice and community service (information on and review of textbooks and workshop for public school teachers; Center for Elected Officials, providing special research assistance to elected black officials; Language Arts Institute, providing inservice training for teachers in newly desegregated schools; and Upward Bound Program).

ALABAMA CONSORTIUM FOR THE DEVELOPMENT OF HIGHER EDUCATION. Lillian C. Manley, Executive Director. P.O. Box 338, Demopolis, Alabama 36732. 205/289-0177.

Alabama A & M University, Normal; Huntington College, Montgomery; Judson College, Marion; Miles College, Birmingham; Stillman College, Tuscaloosa; University of Montevallo, Montevallo; University of Alabama, University, Alabama.

Among major efforts noted by ACDHE are a calendar of events of common interest, a monthly report, profiles of all faculty in member institutions, joint bookings, a Basic Skills Team "to enhance the recruitment and retention of higher risk college freshmen," a joint library card, a communication network for committee meetings, and library facsimile transmission.

ANCHORAGE HIGHER EDUCATION CONSORTIUM. H. F. Janneck, Director. 2651 Providence Avenue, Anchorage, Alaska 99504. 907/279-0508.

University of Alaska, Senior College; University of Alaska, Community College; Alaska Methodist University; all at Anchorage.

AHEC assists the participating schools in cooperative activities involving student mobility, curriculum development, facilities sharing, and in special programs in health education (Continuing Education in Nursing).

ASSOCIATED CHRISTIAN COLLEGES OF OREGON. Lansing W. Bulgin, Provost. 11652 S.W. Pacific Highway, Portland, Oregon 97223. 503/639-6326.

George Fox College, Newberg; Warner Pacific College, Portland.

ACCO is studying a cluster route and the addition of more institutions and is maintaining cooperative programs with Title III monies. Its programs include a joint social work program directed by a shared professor, coordination of the social sciences through joint faculty appointments and joint curriculum development, two national teaching fellowships, a modest amount of faculty travel money, and professional outside counsel on training, guiding, and strengthening the administrative staff.

ASSOCIATED COLLEGES OF CENTRAL KANSAS. Howard W. Johnston, Executive Director. 115 East Marlin, McPherson, Kansas 67460. 316/241-5150.

Bethany College, Lindsborg; Bethel College, North Newton; Kansas Wesleyan University, Salina; McPherson College, Sterling; Tabor College, Hillsboro.

ACCK programs include institutional research and development; learning laboratory and student services—centers for learning skills, ACT testing and consultants, and student leadership workshops; faculty development; curriculum improvement—January interterm programs, cooperative studies, and visiting professors and lecturers; library services, media, and communication; and administrative improvement—institutional management seminars, a consortium development program, and a computer services center.

ASSOCIATED COLLEGES OF THE MID-HUDSON AREA. John R. Jacobson, Executive Director. 12 Vassar Street, Poughkeepsie, New York 12601. 914/471-8923 or 471-8934.

Bard College, Annandale-on-Hudson; Bennett College, Mill-brook; Dutchess Community College, Poughkeepsie; Marist College, Poughkeepsie; Mount Saint Mary College, Newburgh; State University College at New Paltz, New Paltz; Ulster County Community College, Stone Ridge; Vassar College, Poughkeepsie.

The major programs of ACMHA include a biweekly Calendar of Events; a cooperative music program between the Hudson Valley Philharmonic Society and the area colleges; a Higher Education Opportunity Program; an estuary course on the Hudson River; cross-registration with a no-fee system; and community programs, such as recycling, an education center, state and local government internships, the model cities program, and off-campus work-study jobs.

ASSOCIATED COLLEGES OF THE MIDWEST. Dan M. Martin, President. 60 West Walton Street, Chicago, Illinois 60610. 312/664-9580.

Beloit College, Beloit, Wisconsin; Carleton College, Northfield, Minnesota; Coe College, Cedar Rapids, Iowa; Colorado College, Colorado Springs; Cornell College, Mount Vernon, Iowa; Grinnell College, Grinnell, Iowa; Knox College, Galesburg, Illinois; Lawrence University, Appleton, Wisconsin; Macalester College, St, Paul, Minnesota; Monmouth College, Monmouth, Illinois; Ripon College, Ripon, Wisconsin; St. Olaf College, Northfield, Minnesota.

Among its many programs, ACM features international studies—Arabic, Costa Rican, East Asian in Japan and Poona, India; urban studies in Chicago and urban teaching in Chicago public schools; science programs—a semester at Argonne National Laboratory, a geology course in the Rocky Mountains, and a Wilderness Field Station in northern Minnesota; arts and humanities programs—a seminar at the Newberry Library, a New York arts program, and a program of the arts in London and Florence; a periodical bank and service library of approximately two thousand scholarly journals with a photocopy service; a Transitional Year Program, to strengthen basic skills of students with inadequate academic backgrounds; a data bank for institutional research; the single application method; and a Washington, D.C. office to coordinate ACM member interests in Washington.

ASSOCIATED COLLEGES OF THE ST. LAWRENCE VALLEY. Fritz Grupe, Executive Director. 38 Market Street, Potsdam, New York 13676. 315/265-2790.

State University of New York Agricultural and Technical College at Canton; St. Lawrence University, Canton; Clarkson College of

Technology, Potsdam, New York; State University of New York College at Potsdam.

The Associated Colleges include joint activities between admissions officers, including a tour for guidance counselors, publications, and some shared applications; cooperation between computing centers; long-range planning and seminars; and various interinstitutional cultural affairs.

ASSOCIATION OF COLLEGES AND UNIVERSITIES FOR INTERNATIONAL INTERCULTURAL STUDY. Richard N. Bender, Executive Director. c/o the General Board of Education of the Methodist Church, P.O. Box 871, Nashville, Tennessee 37202. 615/327-2727.

Adrian College, Adrian, Michigan; Albright College, Reading, Pennsylvania; American University, Washington, D.C.; Baldwin-Wallace College, Berea, Ohio; Bennett College, Milbrook, New York; Bethune-Cookman College, Daytona Beach, Florida; Birmingham Southern College, Birmingham, Alabama; Brevard College, Brevard, North Carolina; Dillard University, New Orleans, Louisiana; Emory and Henry College, Emory, Virginia; Hendrix College, Conway, Arizona; Huntington College, Montgomery, Alabama; Huston-Tillotson College, Austin, Texas; Indiana Central College, Indianapolis; Kansas Wesleyan University, Salina; Lambuth College, Jackson, Tennessee; MacMurray College, Jacksonville, Illinois; Morningside College, Sioux City, Iowa; Morristown College, Morristown, Tennessee; Mount Union College, Alliance, Ohio; Nebraska Wesleyan, Lincoln; Oklahoma City University, Oklahoma City; Philander-Smith College, Little Rock, Arkansas; Presbyterian College, Clinton, South Carolina; Randolph Macon College, Ashland, Virginia; Rust College, Holly Springs, Massachusetts; Southern Methodist University, Dallas, Texas; Southwestern College, Winfield, Kansas; Southwestern University, Georgetown, Texas; Union College, Lincoln, Nebraska; University of Evansville, Evansville, Indiana; Virginia Wesleyan College, Norfolk; Wesleyan College, Macon, Georgia; Westmar College, LeMars, Iowa; West Virginia Wesleyan University, Buckhannon; Wofford College, Spartanburg, South Carolina.

The on-campus activities of ACUI-IS include curriculum development—workshops, conferences, tapes, films, books; faculty development—conferences, consultations, graduate study support, travel; student assistance—conferences, financial aid, exchange; and sponsorship of three regional institutes of international studies. Foreign-study projects have included student workshops in Mexico City and the Graz

Center in Austria; faculty seminars in India and Yugoslavia; and student seminars in India, Hong Kong, and Africa.

ATLANTA UNIVERSITY CENTER. Prince E. Wilson, Executive Secretary. 594 University Place, S.W., Atlanta, Georgia 30314. 404/522-8980.

Atlanta University, Clark College, Interdenominational Theological Center, Morehouse College, Spelman College; all in Atlanta, Georgia.

Among the continuing cooperative arrangements of AUC are free and open exchange of classes, a single library serving all its members, two computers—one for academic needs and one for administrative needs, a mental health clinic, a coordinated security force, a placement center, a science research institute, a united fund-raising effort in the local metropolitan area, and jointly held professorial chairs.

BOSTON THEOLOGICAL INSTITUTE. Walter D. Wagoner, Director. 99 Brattle Street, Cambridge, Massachusetts 02138. 617/547-0557.

Andover Newton Theological School, Newton Centre; Boston College, Department of Theology, Chestnut Hill; Boston University School of Theology, Boston; Episcopal Theological School, Cambridge; Gordon-Conwell Theological Seminary, South Hamilton; Harvard Divinity School, Cambridge; St. John's Seminary, Brighton; Weston College, Cambridge; all in Massachusetts.

Present programs at BTI include cross-registration, library development, Black studies, student affairs, curricular planning, women's studies, continuing education, administration and governance, and financial development.

BROOKLYN INSTITUTIONAL COUNCIL. Howard Spierer, Staff Director. Hotel Bossert, Suite 829, 98 Montague Street, Brooklyn, New York 11201. 212/624-8100, ext. 829.

Postsecondary institutions: Brooklyn Center, Long Island University; Brooklyn College; Brooklyn Law School; College of Insurance; Kingsborough Community College; Medgar Evers College; New York City Community College; Polytechnic Institute of Brooklyn; Pratt Institute; St. Francis College; St. Joseph's College. Elementary and secondary schools: Brooklyn Friends School; Packer Collegiate Institute; St. Ann's Episcopal School. Recreational and Cultural Institutions: Brooklyn Institute of Arts and Sciences—Brooklyn Botanic Garden, Brooklyn Museum, Children's Museum; Brooklyn Public Library; Young Men's Christian Association—Brooklyn Central Branch; Young

Women's Christian Association. Hospital: Brooklyn Cumberland Medical Center, Brooklyn Hospital.

BIC is exploring cross-registration, sharing of facilities, and joint printing.

CENTRAL PENNSYLVANIA CONSORTIUM. Arden K. Smith, Director of the Consortium. Gettysburg College, Gettysburg, Pennsylvania 17325. 717/334-3131, ext. 323.

Dickinson College, Carlisle; Franklin and Marshall College, Lancaster; Gettysburg College, Gettysburg; Wilson College, Chambersburg.

Among the major programs of CPC are THUS—an urban semester in Harrisburg supported by tuition funds and a grant from IBM; a Southeast Asian Studies program at the University of Mysore in Southern India; a proposed Latin American Studies program at the University of Antioquia in Medellin, Colombia; a summer session —a cooperative effort by member institutions offering credit-interchangeable courses at two of the four campuses; a High School Counselor Visitation Program; meetings to investigate joint purchasing possibilities; and production of a four-college calendar. CPC permits nonmember institutions to affiliate with its programs.

CHICAGO CLUSTER OF THEOLOGICAL SCHOOLS. Robert J. Flinn, Executive Director. 1100 East 55th Street, Chicago, Illinois 60615. 312/ 667-3500.

Bellarmine School of Theology, Chicago; Bethany Theological Seminary, Oakbrook; Catholic Theological Union, Chicago; Chicago Theological Seminary; DeAndreis Seminary, Lemont; Lutheran School of Theology at Chicago; Meadville/Lombard Theological School, Chicago; Northern Baptist Theological Seminary, Oakbrook.

CCTS offers academic and professional degrees at the master's and doctoral levels and programs of continuing education for clergy and laity. Among its achievements are the adoption of a common academic calendar; establishment of cross-registration privileges for course work and supervised clinical placements; exchange of faculty; the sharing of library facilities; establishment of reciprocal library privileges; installation of a teletype communication network and courier service; joint development of policies and procedures for acquisition; the adoption of a common fiscal year; sharing of classrooms, housing facilities, and instructional and office equipment; and common purchasing and joint employment of personnel in plant and food service management.

THE CHICAGO CONSORTIUM OF COLLEGES AND UNIVERSITIES. John M. Beck, Executive Director. 23 East Jackson Boulevard, #1505, Chicago, Illinois 60604. 312/922-3944.

Chicago State University; Concordia Teachers College, River Forest; DePaul University, Chicago; Governors State University, Park Forest South; Loyola University of Chicago; Northeastern Illinois University, Chicago; Roosevelt University, Chicago; University of Illinois, Circle Campus, Chicago.

The Consortium and its participating institutions have been involved primarily in federally funded projects to improve and to innovate programs preparing teachers for inner-city elementary schools. These projects include Teacher Corps, Urban Teacher Corps, Veterans in Education, and TTT (Comprehensive Approach to Restructuring Teacher Education); establishing cooperative student teaching centers in two inner-city public elementary schools in Chicago; conducting a special internship program for experienced employed teachers; and providing professional assistance to several community-based educational organizations.

CHRISTIAN COLLEGE CONSORTIUM. Edward Neteland, Executive Director. 1400 Touhy Avenue, Des Plaines, Illinois 60018. 312/297-7126.

Bethel College, St. Paul, Minnesota; Eastern Mennonite College, Harrisonburg, Virginia; Gordon College, Wenham, Massachusetts; Greenville College, Greenville, Illinois; Malone College, Canton, Ohio; Messiah College, Grantham, Pennsylvania; Seattle Pacific College, Seattle, Washington; Taylor University, Upland, Indiana; Westmont College, Santa Barbara, California; Wheaton College, Wheaton, Illinois.

The CCC is developing a national university system of evangelical christian colleges. Its initial programs include a Distinguished Scholar Program, where a visiting scholar speaks and visits for a day at each campus; a consortium newspaper *Universitas;* exploring joint purchase of fire and liability insurance.

THE CLAREMONT COLLEGES. Howard R. Bowen, Chancellor. Claremont University Center, Harper Hall, Claremont, California 91711. 714/626-8511.

Claremont Graduate School, Claremont Men's College, Claremont University Center, Harvey Mudd College, Pitzer College, Pomona College, Scripps College, all in Claremont, California.

Some of the Claremont College activities are the Honnold Library System; the Human Resources Institute—including a Black Studies Center, a Mexican-American Studies Center, and an Urban and Regional Studies Center; a central business office; a student health service; a counseling center; a computer center; an Office of Institutional Research; a student housing office; and campus security.

CLEVELAND COMMISSION ON HIGHER EDUCATION. W. J. Burns, Executive Director. 1367 East Sixth Street, Cleveland, Ohio 44114. 216/241-7583.

Baldwin-Wallace College, Berea, Ohio; Case Western Reserve University, Cleveland, Ohio; Cuyahoga Community College, Cleveland; John Carroll University, Cleveland; Notre Dame College, Cleveland; Saint John College of Cleveland; the Cleveland State University; Ursuline College, Cleveland.

Among the activities undertaken by CCHE are Project Help—a Ford Foundation grant project to assist Cleveland inner-city high school graduates to continue their educational careers; Project Site—preservice and inservice teacher education coordination; an Admissions Committee; a Cultural Events Committee; a Continuing Education Committee; an Education Committee; and a Study Abroad Committee.

COLLEGE CENTER OF THE FINGER LAKES. Gary H. Quehl, Executive Director. Houghton House, Corning, New York 14830. 607/962-3134.

Alfred University, Alfred, New York; Cazenovia College, Cazenovia, New York; Elmira College, Elmira, New York; Hartwick College, Oneonta, New York.

Priority programs for at least the next three years include complete student access to all on-campus and off-campus programs of the member colleges, as well as to all CCFL-sponsored projects; refinement of the ten-year-old admissions program, including cooperative travel, high school guidance counselors' annual tour to the colleges, and single application method; continuation and probable expansion of the graduate center, which currently offers three master's degrees; the development of a broadly based, multidisciplinary environmental studies program; and a far-reaching faculty development program. CCFL holds title two separate operations: the Graduate Center and the Consortium, both of which contract programs out to nonmember as well as member institutions. Programs featuring a relatively high amount of outside contracting include the Finger Lakes Institute, a year-round environmental research-study center on Seneca Lake, New York; and a Bahamian Project on San Salvador—coordinated field studies in cultural anthropology, botany, marine biology, and archaeology.

COLLEGES OF MID-AMERICA, INC. Everette L. Walker, President. Insurance Exchange Building, Suite 415, Seventh and Pierce, Sioux City, Iowa 51101. 712/277-2260.

Briar Cliff College, Sioux City, Iowa; Buena Vista College, Storm Lake, Iowa; Dakota Wesleyan University, Mitchell, South Dakota; Dordt College, Sioux Center, Iowa; Huron College, Huron, South Dakota; Morningside College, Sioux City, Iowa; Mount Marty College, Yankton, South Dakota; Northwestern College, Orange City, Iowa; Sioux Falls College, Sioux Falls, South Dakota; Westmar College, LeMars, Iowa; Yankton College, Yankton, South Dakota.

Programs and activities of CMA include a monthly newsletter; library union lists and special loan agreements; providing nationally known speakers to enrich faculty development seminars; practicing group purchasing with financial success; a free interinstitutional four-one-four plan; and the gathering and sharing of institutional study data.

COMMITTEE ON INSTITUTIONAL COOPERATION. Frederick H. Jackson, Director. 1603 Orrington Avenue, Suite 970, Evanston, Illinois 60201. 312/866-6630.

Indiana University, Bloomington; Michigan State University, East Lansing; Northwestern University, Evanston, Illinois; Ohio State University, Columbus; Purdue University, Lafayette, Indiana; University of Chicago; University of Illinois, Urbana; University of Iowa, Iowa City; University of Michigan, Ann Arbor; University of Minnesota, Minneapolis; University of Wisconsin, Madison.

CIC is concerned with every aspect of university operations, academic and nonacademic, except athletics. Current interests include educational programs—summer institutes in South Asian and African Languages, MAT in French in France, Spanish in Mexico City, traveling language scholar program, instructional television, summer geology field camp, continuing education in pharmacy and veterinary science, special programs for minorities students in medicine and library science, central library for classic films, Traveling Scholar Program for doctoral candidates; education and research activities—Ocean Sciences program in cooperation with the University of Miami, Environmental Action program, Great Lakes Studies program, cic-Newberry Library programs in the History of Cartography, American Indian studies, and the History of the Family; Polar studies; Research and Development of Instructional Resources; university administration and management —compilation of comparative administrative data, cooperative purchasing, study of university press operations, studies of equal employment opportunity compliance, and support for central periodical bank; educational planning—the time-shortened degree, survey of nontraditional education, microfilm journals publication, faculty evaluation, educational opportunities for itinerant students, and faculty exchange.

CONFERENCE OF RECTORS AND PRINCIPALS OF QUEBEC UNVERSITIES, INC. Rene Hurtubise, General Director. 6600 Chemin de la Cote des Neiges, Suite 300, Montreal 249, Quebec, Canada. 514/342-5696.

McGill University, Montreal; Universite de Montreal; Universite du Quebec a Montreal; Sir George Williams University, Montreal; Bishop's University, Lennoxville, Quebec; Universite Laval, Ste-Foy, Quebec; Universite du Quebec, Quebec; Universite du Quebec a Chicoutimi; Universite du Quebec a Trois-Rivieres; Universite de Sherbrooke, Sherbrooke, Quebec.

Within the Conference, the universities conduct planned, systematic development and coordinate higher education and research, including qualitative evaluation of academic programs, planning teaching methods, student affairs, coordination of libraries, and space-utilization studies.

CONSORTIUM FOR CONTINUING HIGHER EDUCATION IN NORTHERN VIRGINIA. Dean E. Brundage, Director. 4210 Roberts Road, Fairfax, Virginia 22030. 703/323-2155.

George Mason University, Fairfax; Northern Virginia Community College (five campuses), Annandale; University of Virginia, Northern Virginia Regional Center, Falls Church; Virginia Polytechnic Institute and State University, Reston.

The Consortium coordinates the efforts of the member institutions in assessing continuing education needs and in cooperative planning to meet these needs. It also promotes the programs of its member institutions through publications. In the future the Consortium expects to play a significant role in the evaluation of instructional programs, provide educational research services, provide interinstitutional educational counseling, and assume something of an ombudsman role regarding the interests of adult students and the state institutions which serve them.

CONSORTIUM FOR HIGHER EDUCATION RELIGION STUDIES. Frederick Kirschenmann, James H. Legg, Team Directors. 1435 Cornell Drive, Dayton, Ohio 45406. 513/276-3941.

Antioch College, Yellow Springs, Ohio; Ashland Theological Seminary, Wilberforce, Ohio; Central State University, Wilberforce, Ohio; Defiance College, Defiance, Ohio; Earlham School of Religion, Richmond, Indiana; Hamma School of Theology, Springfield, Ohio; Methodist Theological Seminary, Findlay, Ohio; Mt. Saint Mary Seminary of the West, Cincinnati, Ohio; Lutheran Theological Seminary, Columbus, Ohio; Payne Theological Seminary, Wilberforce, Ohio; Pontifical College Josephinum, Worthington, Ohio; St. John Vianney Seminary, Steubenville, Ohio; St. Leonard's College, Centerville, Ohio; St. Mary Seminary, Cleveland, Ohio; United Theological Seminary, Dayton, Ohio; University of Dayton, Dayton, Ohio; Wilberforce University, Wilberforce, Ohio; Wilmington College, Wilmington, Ohio; Winebrenner Theological Seminary, Findlay, Ohio.

Current activities of the consortium include a pilot project in Advanced Education for Ministry, inservice continuing education; development of Foreign Contextual Education; development of a common summer school program; a coordinating common calendar; development of a common catalogue of resources; development of common student aid procedures; research on Black Studies; development of interprofessional training; exploration of common problems in religious education; and library cooperation.

CONSORTIUM OF UNIVERSITIES. John Whalen, Secretary. 1717 Massachusetts Avenue, Washington, D.C. 20036. 202/265-1313.

Charter members: American University, Catholic University of America, George Washington University, Georgetown University, Howard University. Associate members: District of Columbia Teachers College, Dunbarton College, Gallaudet College, Trinity College; all of Washington, D.C.

The Consortium cooperates on potential programs of interinstitutional studies in almost all fields; joint purchasing of helium, nitrogen, and some categories of paper; an intercampus library exchange and delivery system; D.C. Program IMPACT; an Urban Transportation Center, and a D.C. Students-in-Court program, where supervised law students defend indigent persons in landlord-tenant and small claims cases.

COOPERATING RALEIGH COLLEGES. M. Austin Connors, Jr., Director. Meredith College, Raleigh, North Carolina 27611. 919/833-6461.

Meredith College, North Carolina State University, Peace College, St. Augustine's College, St. Mary's College, Shaw University; all of Raleigh North Carolina.

Interinstitutional agreements among CRC members have resulted in cooperation in student interchange for classes; joint use of library facilities; joint catalogue listing of some library materials; faculty seminars; faculty interchange; joint use of faculty; science improvement; joint musical events; and shared use of some facilities.

COOPERATING WINFIELD COLLEGES. Byron E. Moore, Coordinator. St. John's College, Winfield, Kansas 67156. 913/221-4000.

Southwestern College, Winfield, Kansas; St. John's College, Winfield, Kansas; Bi-State Mental Health Foundation, Ponca City, Oklahoma.

The full-time CWC coordinator has direct responsibilities for faculty development, institutional studies, management development, and responsibility for supervision of all other aspects. Programs include joint class scheduling in business, language, and music; a clinical psychologist; a developmental program; a drug education program; and a volunteer telephone hotline operation; and a libraries development program.

COUNCIL FOR HIGHER EDUCATION IN NEWARK. James B. Kelley, Executive Director. 240 High Street, Newark, New Jersey 07102. 210/645-5551.

College of Medicine and Dentistry of New Jersey-New Jersey Medical School, Essex County College, Newark College of Engineering, Rutgers–The State University, all at Newark, New Jersey.

CHEN members work together to establish joint use of facilities as well as interrelated programs, particularly in health sciences, graduate studies, and in areas of direct relevance to Newark.

COUNCIL FOR INTERCULTURAL STUDIES AND PROGRAMS. Ward Morehouse, President. Foreign Area Materials Center, 60 East 42nd Street, New York, New York 10017. 212/972-9877.

Associated Colleges of the Midwest, Chicago, Illinois; Center for International Programs and Comparative Studies, Albany, New York; Central States College Association, Rock Island, Illinois; Cincinnati Council on World Affairs, Cincinnati, Ohio; College Center of the Finger Lakes, Corning, New York; Great Lakes Colleges Association, Ann Arbor, Michigan; Indiana Consortium on International Programs, Terre Haute, Indiana; Kansas City Regional Council for Higher Education, Kansas City, Missouri; Montana Association for International Studies, Bozeman, Montana; Regional Council for International Education, Pittsburgh, Pennsylvania; Southern Atlantic States Association for South Asian Studies Davidson, North Carolina; University Center in Virginia, Richmond, Virginia; Vermont Council on World Affairs, Burlington, Vermont.

cisp is a cooperative association of educational organizations and institutions to strengthen the transnational and intercultural concerns of the learning community of students and teachers, primarily at the undergraduate level. Some activities of the council are an intercultural studies information service; consultative services; conferences; self-instruction in critical languages; strengthening the teaching of Asian religions and philosophies; population studies; innovation in undergraduate education; and a Foreign Area Materials Center.

COUNCIL OF HIGHER EDUCATIONAL INSTITUTIONS IN NEW YORK CITY. Robert L. Lincoln, Executive Director. 461 Park Avenue South, New York, New York 10016. 212/683-3500.

Academy of Aeronautics, Bank Street College of Education, Cathedral College of the Immaculate Conception, City University of New York, College for Human Services, College of Insurance, College of Mount St. Vincent, Columbia University (three campuses), Finch College, Hebrew Union College, Juilliard School of Music, Long Island University (three campuses), M. J. Lewi College of Podiatry, Manhattan College, Manhattan School of Music, Mannes College of Music, Marymount Manhattan College, New York Institute of Technology (two campuses), Rockefeller University, St. Francis College, St. Joseph's College, State University of New York (three campuses), Touro College, Voorhees Technical Institute, Wagner College, Yeshiva University (three campuses); all of New York City.

The Council has sponsored the development of an instructional television program, a study of library research in New York City, and the cooperative use of libraries, a study of the cooperative use of data processing, various seminars and administrative studies.

COUNCIL OF ONTARIO UNIVERSITIES. John B. Macdonald, Executive Director. 102 Bloor Street West, Toronto, Ontario, Canada. 416/920-6865.

Brock University, Carleton University, University of Guelph, Lakehead University, Laurentian University of Sudbury, McMaster University, Universite d'Ottawa, Queen's University at Kingston, University of Toronto, Trent University, University of Waterloo, University of Western Ontario, University of Windsor, York University; all of Ontario.

The Council's activities include studies of operating and capital financing, the planning of development of graduate studies in the province, coordination of admissions, library cooperation, development of a computer network, instructional development, and miscellaneous research studies.

DAYTON-MIAMI VALLEY CONSORTIUM. Charles J. Armstrong, President. 300 College Park Avenue, Dayton, Ohio 45409. 513/224-1204.

Institutional Members: Air Force Institute of Technology, Dayton; Antioch College, Yellow Springs; Cedarville College, Cedarville; Central State University, Wilberforce; Clark Technical College, Springfield; School of the Dayton Art Institute, Dayton; University of Dayton, Dayton; Sinclair Community College, Dayton; Urbana College, Urbana; Wilberforce University, Wilberforce; Wilmington College, Wilmington; Wittenberg University, Springfield; Wright State University, Dayton. Associate Members: Cox Heart Institute, Kettering; Engineering and Science Institute of Dayton; Frigidaire Division, General Motors Corp., Dayton; Charles F. Kettering Foundation, Dayton; Miami Valley Regional Planning Commission, Dayton; Model Cities Planning Council of Dayton, Ohio, Inc., Dayton; National Cash Register Co., Dayton.

DMVC operates in two broad areas: community service and interinstitutional cooperation. Community service activities include Urban Corps, involving approximately 250 DMVC students; VISTA, including a University Year in Action proposal; Model Cities Training Institute; a Model Cities Educational Facility—Feasibility Study; Faculty Utilization of Urban Resources project; Metropolitan Programs Center; and a Public Opinion Center involving many DMVC students in information gathering.

General consortium activities include limited Cross-registration; education television, with planning to operate joint education facility;

a Headstart Supplementary Training Program; a Faculty Data Bank; joint purchasing of Xerox toner and paper; an advanced professional program in engineering; and library cooperation with a union list for the forty-four area libraries, interlibrary loaning, and photography.

EAST CENTRAL COLLEGE CONSORTIUM. Elmer Jagow, Chairman. Hiram College, Hiram, Ohio 44234. 216/569-3211. Washington Office: Flora B. Harper. Suite 810, 1028 Connecticut Avenue, N.W., Washington, D.C. 20036. 202/659-4112.

Bethany College, Bethany, West Virginia; Heidelberg College, Tiffin, Ohio; Hiram College, Hiram, Ohio; Marietta College, Marietta, Ohio; Mount Union College, Alliance, Ohio; Muskingum College, New Concord, Ohio; Westminster College, New Wilmington, Pennsylvania.

The Washington Office keeps the member colleges fully informed of federal programs in higher education, assists faculty and administration in presenting educational projects for federal funding, and represents the principles and goals of the Consortium before Washington-based organizations. The Consortium also undertakes student and faculty exchanges; conferences of students, faculty, and staff on mutual problems; Washington internships for students; and the exchange of statistical data.

EISENHOWER CONSORTIUM FOR WESTERN ENVIRONMENTAL FORESTRY RESEARCH. Dean R. E. Dils, President. College of Forestry and Natural Resources, Office of the Dean, Colorado State University, Fort Collins, Colorado 80521. 303/491-6542.

Northern Arizona University, Flagstaff, Arizona; Arizona State University, Tempe, Arizona; University of Arizona, Tucson, Arizona; Colorado State University, Fort Collins, Colorado; University of Colorado, Boulder, Colorado; New Mexico State University, Las Cruces, New Mexico; University of New Mexico, Albuquerque, New Mexico; Texas Tech University, Lubbock, Texas; University of Wyoming, Laramie, Wyoming; United States Forest Service Rocky Mountain Forest and Range Experiment Station, Fort Collins, Colorado.

The Consortium combines and coordinates the research efforts of interested educational institutions and the Forest Service to solve the problems of man and his interactions with the environment. It selects problems, formulates research programs, solicits research proposals to implement these programs, and provides the machinery through which Forest Service research grants are made to universities.

FIVE COLLEGES, INCORPORATED. North Burn, Coordinator. Box 740, Amherst, Massachusetts 01002. 413/256-8316.

Amherst College, Amherst; Hampshire College, Amherst; Mount Holyoke College, South Hadley; Smith College, Northampton; University of Massachusetts, Amherst; all of Massachusetts.

Among the programs operated by Five Colleges, Incorporated are student interchange at no additional charge; Five College bus; faculty interchange; academic coordination—joint course listing, area programs; cooperative astronomy department; cooperative Ph.D. program; Hampshire Inter-Library Center—joint depository for expensive, but relatively little-used books and periodicals; Five College Radio— WFCR-FM, a noncommerical educational radio station; *The Massachusetts Review*—a quarterly journal of literature and public affairs; a calendar of events; and a registry of part-time workers.

GREAT LAKES COLLEGES ASSOCIATION. Lawrence Barrett, acting president, 555 East William, Ann Arbor, Michigan 48108. 313/761-4833.

Albion College, Albion, Michigan; Antioch College, Yellow Springs, Ohio; College of Wooster, Wooster, Ohio; Denison University, Granville, Ohio; DePauw University, Greencastle, Indiana; Earlham College, Richmond, Indiana; Hope College, Holland, Michigan; Kalamazoo College, Kalamazoo, Michigan; Kenyon College, Gambier, Ohio; Oberlin College, Oberlin, Ohio; Ohio Wesleyan University, Delaware, Ohio; Wabash College, Crawfordsville, Indiana.

GLCA operates almost wholly off-campus programs, among which are Africa—both French-speaking and English-speaking; European term on comparative urban studies, with an emphasis on the experiments on new towns; India—five university centers; Latin America (Colombia); Japan; Middle East (Israel and Lebanon); Scotland; Taiwan; USSR; and Yugoslavia—a summer program and developing a full semester program. Its United States studies include a New York Arts Program, an Oak Ridge Science Semester, and a Philadelphia Urban Semester.

GREATER HARTFORD CONSORTIUM FOR HIGHER EDUCATION, INC. Robert M. Vogel, Executive Director. 201 Bloomfield Avenue, West Hartford, Connecticut 06117. 203/233-1553.

Hartford College for Women, Hartford; Rensselaer Polytechnic Institute of Connecticut, Hartford; St. Joseph College, West Hartford; Trinity College, Hartford; University of Hartford, West Hartford.

The Greater Hartford Consortium offers it members an intercampus registration program, augmented by a shuttle bus; inventory exchanges on expensive laboratory equipment and of special library holdings; and several projected joint academic programs.

GREENSBORO TRI-COLLEGE CONSORTIUM. William J. Lanier, Director. 501 West Washington Street, Greensboro, North Carolina 27402. 919/ 275-5395.

Bennett College, Greensboro College, Guilford College, all of Greensboro, North Carolina.

The major programs of the consortium include one-third time library coordinator; one-third time secretary; shared clinical psychologist; shuttle-bus service for students and library materials; curriculum workshops in history, elementary education, physical education and earth science, considering coordinated and shared course offerings; cooperative offerings of low-enrollment courses; no-fee student interchange; joint course numbering; joint cultural events; and computer cooperation.

GROUP TEN COMMUNITY COLLEGES FOR THE SEVENTIES. Herbert H. Wood, Executive Director. 4100 Connecticut Avenue, N.W., Washington, D.C. 20008. 202/629-7870.

Brevard Junior College, Cocoa, Florida; Chabot College, Hayward, California; Essex County College, Newark, New Jersey; Metropolitan Junior College District, Kansas City, Missouri; Monterey Peninsula College, Monterey, California; Tarrant County Junior College, Fort Worth, Texas; Washington Technical Institute, Washington, D.C.; William Rainey Harper College, Palatine, Illinois.

GT/70 programs include workshops in curriculum development, instructional media, student services and management. A unique means of information sharing through use of video tapes is now in operation. A daily Who is Doing What information system reports on faculty development, career education curricula and counseling, individualized instruction, and management improvement.

HIGHER EDUCATION CENTER FOR URBAN STUDIES. H. Parker Lansdale, Director. 328 Park Avenue, Bridgeport, Connecticut 06604. 203/384-0711, ext. 634.

Bridgeport Engineering Institute, Bridgeport; Fairfield University, Fairfield; Housatonic Community College, Stratford; Sacred Heart University, Bridgeport; University of Bridgeport; all in Connecticut.

HECUS was formed to coordinate urban-oriented projects in the Greater Bridgeport area. Its premier programs include running an urban corps in Greater Bridgeport, CONNCORD (Connecticut Consortium on Research Development) a provider of research support, Model Cities, and a Higher Education Opportunities Program to recruit students from the Model Cities area, an Environmental Studies Institute.

HIGHER EDUCATION COORDINATING COUNCIL OF METROPOLITAN ST. LOUIS. Francis C. Gamelin, Executive Director. 5600 Oakland Avenue, Rooms F313-319, St. Louis, Missouri 63110. 314/644-6613.

Cooperating School Districts of the St. Louis Suburban Area; Fontbonne College, St. Louis; Harris Teachers College, St. Louis; Lindenwood College, St. Charles, Missouri; Maryville College, St. Louis; St. Louis College of Pharmacy; St. Louis-St. Louis County Junior College District; St. Louis Public Schools; St. Louis University; Southern Illinois University, Edwardsville, Illinois; University of Missouri at St. Louis; Washington University, St. Louis; Webster College, St. Louis.

Current activities of HECC are conducted through committees representative of participating colleges and universities and, in some instances, appropriate community agencies. Longstanding committees include library, graduate education, student teaching, computer, admissions, and television committees. Plans now are being formulated for cooperative graduate work, sophistication of learning resources, and faculty interaction.

HUDSON-MOHAWK ASSOCIATION OF COLLEGES AND UNIVERSITIES. Robert M. Briber, Executive Director. 356 Troy-Schenectady Road, Latham, New York 12110. 518/785-3219.

Albany College of Pharmacy; Albany Law School; Albany Medical College; The College of Saint Rose, Albany; Rensselaer Polytechnic Institute, Troy; Russell Sage College, Troy; Siena College, Loudonville; Skidmore College, Saratoga Springs; Union College, Schenectady.

The Hudson-Mohawk Association has established several programs in student cross-registration, a series of "Consortium Night" courses one night per week, and several "cluster catalogues" which list all offerings in certain fields. There has been cooperation among the academic deans, admissions officers, business officers, computer center directors, continuing education directors, development officers, placement officers, and faculty groups.

INTERUNIVERSITY COUNCIL OF THE NORTH TEXAS AREA. R. C. Peavey, Interim Executive Director. 2400 North Armstrong Parkway, Richardson, Texas 75080. 214/231-7211.

Corporate institutions: East Texas State University, Commerce; North Texas State University, Denton; Southern Methodist University, Dallas; Texas Christian University, Fort Worth; University of Texas at Arlington; University of Texas Southwestern Medical School, Dallas; University of Dallas. Member institutions: Austin College, Sherman; Bishop College, Dallas; Dallas Baptist College; Texas Wesleyan College, Fort Worth. Affiliate Member Institutions: Baylor University College of Dentistry, Dallas; University of Texas at Dallas.

IUC has programs in interinstitutional cooperation and planning in graduate study, research, utilization of library facilities, a cooperative library program with daily courier service, a private-line teletype system, a common library courtesy card for faculty and all graduate students, and a document exchange program for surplus library materials, principally periodicals and/or serials.

INTER-UNIVERSITY INSTITUTE OF ENGINEERING CONTROL. D. J. Hollister, Secretary. University College of North Wales, School of Engineering Science, Dean Street, Bangor, Caerns, Wales, England. Bangor 51151.

School of Engineering Science, University College of North Wales, Bangor, Caernavonshire; School of Applied Science, University of Sussex, Falmer, Brighton; Department of Engineering Science, University of Warwick, Coventry.

The Inter-University Institute of Engineering Control promotes and coordinates research in the field of automatic control engineering, and promotes cost effectiveness in this area by sharing resources and eliminating unnecessary duplication, especially in the areas of distributed parameter systems, and engine, vehicle and transport systems. The Institute also provides a master's course in control engineering.

KANSAS CITY REGIONAL COUNCIL FOR HIGHER EDUCATION. Lloyd J. Averill, President. 4901 Main Street, Suite 309, Kansas City, Missouri 64112. 816/561-6693.

Avila College, Kansas City; Baker University, Baldwin, Kansas; Benedictine College, Atchison, Kansas; Donnelly College, Kansas City, Kansas; Graceland College, Lamoni, Iowa; Kansas City Art Institute, Kansas City; Kansas City Kansas Community Junior College, Kansas

City; Metropolitan Junior College District, Kansas City; Missouri Valley College, Marshall; Ottawa University, Ottawa, Kansas; Park College, Parkville; Rockhurst College, Kansas City; Saint Mary College, Leavenworth, Kansas; Tarkio College, Tarkio; University of Missouri at Kansas City; William Jewell College, Liberty, Missouri.

Among the shared resources and programs of KCRCHE are a joint telephone network; library cooperation—joint periodicals, microfilm, interlibrary lending agreement, joint catalogue, and special collections; a limited student exchange agreement; shared use of computers; a Cooperative Social Welfare Action Program; Summer Field courses in American Indian Reservations; inner-city Teacher Preparation semester; cooperative Insurance programs; and long-range planning.

KENTUCKIANA METROVERSITY. John H. Ford, Coordinator. 9001 Shelbyville Road, Louisville, Kentucky 40222. 502/425-8261.

Bellarmine College, Louisville; Indiana University Southeast, Jeffersonville; Louisville Presbyterian Seminary; Southern Baptist Theological Seminary, Louisville; Spalding College, Louisville; University of Louisville.

Students attending a member institution of the Metroversity may take courses at other members institutions, obtain dual degrees, and may borrow books from any library of member institutions. Another major program of Kentuckiana Metroversity is CHOPS (Community Health Orientation Program for Students)—a pilot educational program in community health for an interdisciplinary team of students.

LAKE SUPERIOR ASSOCIATION OF COLLEGES AND UNIVERSITIES. F. X. Shea, Chairman of the Board. College of St. Scholastica, Duluth, Minnesota 55811. 218/728-5885.

Lakehead University, Thunder Bay, Ontario; University of Minnesota, Duluth; University of Wisconsin at Superior; Northland College, Ashland, Wisconsin; Mt. Senario College, Ladysmith, Wisconsin; College of St. Scholastica, Duluth, Minnesota.

The Lake Superior Association plans to collaborate and pool resources in minority and Indian studies, public service activities, libaries, instructional media, convocations, fine arts, environmental studies and research with special references to the Lake Superior Basin, health sciences, faculty and student exchange, continuing education, international programs, U.S.-Canadian relations, summer programs, cross registration, and joint graduate and continuing educational programs.

LEAGUE FOR INNOVATION IN THE COMMUNITY COLLEGE. B. Lamar Johnson, Executive Director. 1100 Glendon Avenue, Westwood Center, Suite 925, Los Angeles, California 90024. 213/477-7255.

Brookdale Community College, Lincroft, New Jersey; Central Piedmont Community College, Charlotte, North Carolina; Coast Community College District, Costa Mesa, California; Cuyahoga Community College, Cleveland, Ohio; Dallas County Community Junior College District, Dallas, Texas; Delta College, University Center, Michigan; Foothill Community Junior College District, Los Altos Hills, California; Junior College District, St. Louis, Missouri; Kern Community College District, Bakersfield, California; Los Angeles Community College District, Los Angeles, California; Los Rios Community College District, Sacramento, California; Maricopa County Community College District, Phoenix, Arizona; Moraine Valley Community College, Palos Hills, Illinois; Peralta Community College District, Oakland, California; Santa Fe Junior College, Gainesville, Florida.

The League seeks to accomplish its purposes by cooperative work among its members which assists them to experiment in teaching, learning, guidance and other aspects of junior college operation; share results of experiments; share conceptual planning and learning objectives; exchange instructional materials and procedures designed to enhance learning; examine the relevance of varied modes of college administration to experimentation in teaching and learning; provide a common base for research on the effects of varied innovative practices by gathering and sharing data on students, programs, and modes of organization; and evaluate the impact of the institution's practices on its students and community.

LEHIGH VALLEY ASSOCIATION OF INDEPENDENT COLLEGES. Mahlon H. Hellerick, Coordinator. 87 West Church Street, Bethlehem, Pennsylvania 18018. 215/691-6131.

Allentown College, Center Valley; Cedar Crest College, Allentown; Lafayette College, Easton; Lehigh University, Bethlehem; Moravian College, Bethlehem; Muhlenberg College, Allentown.

Among the present programs of the Lehigh Valley Association of Independent Colleges are a cross-registration policy; reciprocity in student admission to cultural programs; an interlibrary loan system in which the libraries are linked by a TWX line; an interinstitutional program in social welfare education; development of a computer network linking all six colleges; and cooperative administration of summer session programs.

THE MARINE SCIENCE CONSORTIUM, INC. B. L. Oostdam, President. P.O. Box 43, Millersville, Pennsylvania 17551. 717/872-5411, ext. 304 or 451.

Bloomsburg State College, Bloomsburg; California State College, California; Catholic University of America, Washington, D.C.; Cheyney State College, Cheyney; East Stroudsburg State College, East Stroudsburg; Edinboro State College, Edinboro; Indiana University of Pennsylvania, Indiana; Kutztown State College, Kutztown; Millersville State College, Millersville; Penn State University, University Park; Shippensburg State College, Shippensburg; Slippery Rock State College, Slippery Rock; West Chester State College, West Chester; West Virginia University, Morgantown, West Virginia.

The Marine Science Consortium operates the Delaware Bay Marine Science Center in Lewes, Delaware and the Wallops Island Marine Science Center in Virginia. Principal programs include a summer session, a Pre-College Oceanography Program, a one-week oceanography minicruise, and general research activities.

MID-AMERICA STATE UNIVERSITIES ASSOCIATION. Paul M. Young, Executive Director. 108 Anderson Hall, Kansas State University, Manhattan, Kansas 66502. 913/532-6221.

Iowa State University, Ames; Kansas State University, Manhattan; Oklahoma State University, Stillwater; University of Kansas, Lawrence; University of Missouri, Columbia, Rolla, Kansas City, St. Louis; University of Nebraska, Lincoln; University of Oklahoma, Norman.

The ongoing activity at MASUA is the Traveling Scholar Program for Graduate Students, which permits students who are nearing completion of their doctorates to participate at another member institution for one semester. The graduate deans involved must concur, and the student registers and pays his fees at his home institution.

MID-APPALACHIA COLLEGE COUNCIL, INC. Jack E. Snider, Executive Director. P.O. Box 391, Bristol, Tennessee 37620. 615/764-3642.

Carson-Newman College, Jefferson City, Tennessee; Cumberland College, Williamsburg, Kentucky; Emory and Henry College,

Emory, Virginia; King College, Bristol, Tennessee; Knoxville College, Knoxville, Tennessee; Lincoln Memorial University, Harrogate, Tennessee; Maryville College, Maryville, Tennessee; Milligan College, Milligan College, Tennessee; Morristown College, Morristown, Tennessee; Pikeville College, Pikeville, Kentucky; Tusculum College, Greeneville, Tennessee; Union College, Barbourville, Kentucky.

The Council lists as its particular successes a common depository for teaching tapes and films; a lyceum program; an interinstitutional library program including a union list of periodicals; an Office of Education contract to discover talented and impoverished youth in the mountains and motivate them to continue their education; and a field biology research and training facility on Norris Lake.

MIDWEST UNIVERSITIES CONSORTIUM FOR INTERNATIONAL ACTIVITIES, INC. George H. Axinn, Executive Director. 200 Center for International Programs, Michigan State University, East Lansing, Michigan 48823. 517/353-9696.

University of Illinois, Urbana/Champaign; Indiana University, Bloomington; Michigan State University, East Lansing; University of Minnesota, Minneapolis; University of Wisconsin, Madison.

In addition to its visiting scholar program, MUCIA assists member universities in providing more effective technical assistance abroad and in gathering valuable feedback from overseas programs and supports proposals which focus on significant problems, issues, or processes of international development. Other MUCIA programs support library acquisitions, evaluation studies, and interuniversity bodies focusing on major concerns related to problems of underdevelopment.

NASHVILLE UNIVERSITY CENTER. Richard H. Morgan, Executive Director. Fisk University, Box 8, Nashville, Tennessee 37203. 615/329-1676.

Fisk University, Meharry Medical College, George Peabody College for teachers, Scarritt College for Christian Workers, Vanderbilt University, all of Nashville, Tennessee.

The accomplishments of NUC are as follows: putting together an annual fine arts festival by four of the institutions, printing a complete catalogue of fine arts courses across institutional lines, operating a shuttle-bus, developing of a very active Interuniversity Psychology Consortium, facilitating interuniversity library use, establishing a common calendar for the academic year, proposing and getting partially accepted an interuniversity linguistics major, and obtaining funding by the State Department of a program to facilitate interinstitutional cooperation in international exchange. NUC fosters a climate of communication and cooperation which have resulted in the Mater 1 and child health/family planning program, based at Meharry but involving the other NUC institutions, the joint listing of courses in the bulletins of Fisk faculty between the economics departments of Fisk and Vanderbilt, and the agreements between Vanderbilt and Peabody about specialization in the fine arts.

NASSAU HIGHER EDUCATION CONSORTIUM. William M. Heston, Executive Director. 393 Front Street, Hempstead, New York 11550. 516/560-3855.

Adelphi University, Garden City; Hofstra University, Hempstead; Nassau Community College, Garden City; New York Institute of Technology, Old Westbury and New York; C.W. Post Center of Long Island University, Greenvale; Molloy College, Rockville Centre; State University of New York College at Old Westbury, Oyster Bay.

NHEC is working with the State University of New York in developing the minimaster plan for the university institutions on Long Island. It is developing a common academic calendar; a data base for planning purposes for all Long Island institutions—involving student flows, institutional profiles, and finances; task forces on the computer, the County Performing Arts Center at Mitchel Field, faculty fringe benefits and insurance programs, communications programs, a common career and job placement center; and student health services.

NEW HAMPSHIRE COLLEGE AND UNIVERSITY COUNCIL. Henry W. Munroe, Executive Director. 2321 Elm Street, Manchester, New Hampshire 03104. 603/623-1953.

Colby Junior College, New London; Franklin Pierce College, Rindge; Keene State College, Keene; Mount Saint Mary College, Hooksett; New England College, Henniker; Notre Dame College, Manchester; Plymouth State College, Plymouth; Rivier College, Nashua; Saint Anselm's College, Manchester; University of New Hampshire, Durham.

NHCUC members participate in curriculum coordination, interlibrary cooperation, faculty exchanges, and inter-campus seminars. A computer network has been developed among the colleges. By pooling faculty and laboratory resources, the colleges have developed a remarkable Marine Sciences Program.

NEW ORLEANS CONSORTIUM. Mary H. Ellis, Coordinator. Palmetto and Pine Streets, New Orleans, Louisiana 70125. 504/482-1325.

Loyola University, St. Mary's Dominican College, Xavier University, all of New Orleans.

Through the New Orleans Consortium cross-registration up to six hours is available at no extra cost to the student, and students and faculty have access to all library facilities. Other programs include a joint major in Social Welfare; a course on Small Business Operation and Management; and staffing a joint Mental Health program. The Consortium serves as a vehicle for administrative planning and cooperative ventures between the member institutions.

NORTHEAST FLORIDA COOPERATIVE EDUCATION CONSORTIUM. William D. Ceely, Director. Florida Junior College at Jacksonville, Jacksonville, Florida 32205. 904/387-8288.

Central Florida Community College, Ocala; Florida Junior College at Jacksonville; Lake City Community College, Lake City; St. Johns River Junior College, Palatka; Brevard Community College, Cocoa (observer status).

The first year objectives of this consortium of community colleges were to refine planning procedures; test the feasibility of involving physically handicapped persons in cooperative experiences; develop transition programs for veterans as a predischarge procedure and involve them in civilian roles while in service; evaluate scheduling patterns suitable for community college student and institution needs; articulate with high schools and receiving institutions to ease student entry into cooperative study at various levels of education; employ location theory to determine most appropriate job areas for students; and improve communication, management, and evaluation procedures.

NORTHERN PLAINS CONSORTIUM. E. Robert Adkins, Director. Jamestown College, Jamestown, North Dakota 58401. 701/252-4331.

Dickinson State College, Dickinson; Jamestown College, Jamestown; Mary College, Bismark; Mayville State College, Mayville; Minot State College, Minot; Valley City State College, Valley City; all of North Dakota.

The cooperative programs of NPC frequently include many non-member institutions in the area. One of its most successful programs was a development of research project.

OREGON INDEPENDENT COLLEGES ASSOCIATION, INC. Jim Sullivan, Executive Director. Lewis and Clark College, LC Box 196, Portland, Oregon 97219. 503/246-2415.

Columbia Christian College, Portland; Concordia College, Portland; George Fox College, Newberg; Lewis and Clark College, Portland; Linfield College, McMinnville; Marylhurst College, Marylhurst; Mt. Angel College, Mt. Angel; Mt. Angel Seminary, St. Benedict; Museum Art School, Portland; Northwest Christian College, Eugene; Pacific University, Forest Grove; Reed College, Portland; University of Portland, Portland; Warner Pacific College, Portland; Willamette University, Salem.

OICA and the Northwest Association of Private Colleges and Universities, Inc. have two programs for overseas study—one sponsored by each organization—and an extensive library cooperative program involving both the regional state schools and community colleges. One central microfilm center for all the schools has been established. Other activities of OICA include joint hiring of faculty, especially in some of the smaller departments; limited cross-registration for students; joint purchasing and use of administration; extensive and varied cultural programs; and joint recruiting and cooperative advertising for prospective students.

PIEDMONT UNIVERSITY CENTER OF NORTH CAROLINA.   Paul A. Marrotte, Executive Director. Reynolda House, Box 11045, Bethabara Station, Winston-Salem, North Carolina 27106. 919/723-3611.

Barber-Scotia College, Concord; Belmont-Abbey College, Belmont; Bennett College, Greensboro; Catawba College, Salisbury; Davidson College, Davidson; Elon College, Elon College; Greensboro College, Greensboro; Guilford College, Greensboro; High Point College, High Point; Johnson C. Smith College, Charlotte; Lenoir Rhyne College, Hickory; Livingstone College, Salisbury; Mars Hill College, Mars Hill; North Carolina A & T State University, Greensboro; Pfeiffer College, Misenheimer; Queens College, Charlotte; St. Andrews Presbyterian College, Laurinburg; Salem College, Winston-Salem; Wake Forest University, Winston-Salem; Winston-Salem State University, Winston-Salem.

Each program area at PUC is overseen by a separate committee composed of institutional representatives. Among the committees currently active and the programs they oversee are the following: Business Managers—discussion of mutual problems and centralization of NDEA loans; Communications Media—the Film Library—a major program of PUC featuring over two hundred reels of educational film; Faculty

Research—provides grants upon application by faculty members of member institutions; Fine Arts—runs a student art competition for cash prizes; Library Affairs—both cooperative programs and a joint purchasing plan; Teacher Education—workshops on certification, urban teaching, student teaching; and Visiting Scholars.

PINCHOT INSTITUTE (or THE CONSORTIUM FOR ENVIRONMENTAL FORESTRY RESEARCH). Elwood L. Shafer, Northeast Forestry Experiment Station, 6816 Market, Upper Darby, Pennsylvania. 215/597-3749.

Cornell University, Ithaca, New York; Massachusetts Agriculture Experiment Station, Amherst, Massachusetts; Northeast Forestry Experiment Station, Upper Darby, Pennsylvania; Princeton University, Princeton, New Jersey; Rutgers University, New Brunswick, New Jersey; State University of New York at Syracuse; University of Connecticut, Storrs; University of New Hampshire, Durham; Yale University, New Haven, Connecticut.

The Pinchot Institute specializes in urban environmental forestry. The Forest Service funds the consortium, with half the money going to in-house Forestry Service research at the Upper Darby, Pennsylvania facility, and the other half going in grants to the participating institutions for studies selected by the executive committee. Each member may eventually have an experimental laboratory established on its campus under the program.

PITTSBURGH COUNCIL ON HIGHER EDUCATION. J. G. K. Miller, Executive Director. 222 Craft Avenue, Pittsburgh, Pennsylvania 15213. 412/683-7905.

Carlow College, Carnegie-Mellon University, Chatham College, Duquesne University, Point Park College, University of Pittsburgh, all of Pittsburgh.

Among the programs undertaken by PCHE are cross-registration; public information—about PCHE and its programs; a study of possibilities in continuing education and the external degree; library access —programs for interlibrary loans, common cataloguing, and a Union List of Periodicals; and *Viewbook*, a joint publication—"Why Study in Pittsburgh"—sent out to college guidance counselors.

QUAD-CITIES GRADUATE STUDY CENTER. Donald A. Johnson, Director. 639 38th Street, Rock Island, Illinois 61201. 309/794-7376.

Augustana College, Rock Island, Illinois; Iowa State University, Ames; Marycrest College, Davenport, Iowa; Northern Illinois

University, DeKalb; Southern Illinois University, Carbondale-Edwardsville; University of Illinois, Urbana-Champaign; University of Iowa, Iowa City; University of Northern Iowa, Cedar Falls; Western Illinois University, Macomb.

The member institutions of Quad-Cities coordinate all their graduate offerings. The institutions retain the admissions responsibilities as well as the conferral of degree. The master's degrees currently available are in business, economics, education, English and engineering.

REGIONAL COUNCIL FOR INTERNATIONAL EDUCATION.   Joseph J. Malon, President. 1101 Bruce Hall, University of Pittsburgh, Pittsburgh, Pennsylvania 15213. 412/621-7215.

Allegheny College, Meadville, Pennsylvania; Baldwin-Wallace College, Berea, Ohio; Bethany College, Bethany, West Virginia; California State College, California, Pennsylvania; Capital University, Columbus, Ohio; Clarion State College, Clarion, Pennsylvania; Concord College, Athens, West Virginia; Fairmont State College, Fairmont, West Virginia; Findlay College, Findlay, Ohio; Glenville State College, Glenville, West Virginia; Hiram College, Hiram, Ohio; Indiana University of Pennsylvania, Indiana, Pennsylvania; Kent State University, Kent, Ohio; Marshall University, Huntington, West Virginia; Ohio Dominican College, Columbus; Ohio Northern University, Ada; Otterbein College, Westerville, Ohio; Potomac State College, Keyser, West Virginia; Slippery Rock State College, Slippery Rock, Pennsylvania; University of Akron, Akron, Ohio; University of Pittsburgh; Waynesburg College, Waynesburg, Pennsylvania; Westminster College, Waynesburg, Pennsylvania; West Virginia Wesleyan College, Buckhannon; Wilmington College, Wilmington, Ohio; Wittenberg University, Springfield, Ohio.

The principal efforts of RCIE are the Faculty Institute for International Studies, summer seminars overseas for faculty, and the availability of RCIE foreign Scholars-in-Residence to member schools for teaching and lecturing. For students RCIE maintains study centers in Basel, Switzerland, and Verona, Italy; conducts study programs in Cuernavaca, Mexico, and in Japan; holds student institutes, roughly similar to the Faculty Institute for International Studies, several times a year at various sites within the consortium; assists members to conduct intercultural workshops for foreign and American students; and provides assistance to members in processing foreign applicants for admission and in improving foreign student programing. RCIE also engages in research and publishing on international education and intercultural communications, and serves as a national information center on intercultural communications programs.

ROCHESTER AREA COLLEGES. Alexander R. Cameron, Executive Director. 50 West Main Street, Rochester, New York 14614. 716/454-2386.

Colgate Rochester/Bexley Hall Divinity, Rochester; Community College of the Finger Lakes, Canandaigua; Eisenhower College, Seneca Falls; Empire State College, Rochester; Genesee Community College, Batavia; Hobart and William Smith Colleges, Geneva; Keuka College, Keuka Park; Monroe Community College, Rochester; Nazareth College, Rochester; Roberts Wesleyan College, Rochester; Rochester Institute of Technology, Rochester; St. John Fisher College, Rochester; State University College, Brockport; State University College, Geneseo; University of Rochester, Rochester.

RAC intends to develop plans for member colleges to share resources in order that the distinctive strengths in each of the institutions can be economically directed to a high quality of educational opportunity. Also of prime importance is the development of a voluntary, regional plan as a guide for the coordination of higher education so the distinctive missions of each of the colleges can be fitted together.

SAN FRANCISCO CONSORTIUM. Richard Sax, Executive Director. Balboa Building, Suite 516, 593 Market Street, San Francisco, California 94105. 415/392-3502.

City College of San Francisco; Golden Gate College; Hastings College of Law; Lone Mountain College; San Francisco State University; University of California, San Francisco; University of San Francisco.

SFC emphasizes the urban environment and provides special services to minority and disadvantaged students attending its member institutions. Among the projects undertaken by SFC are a Minority Student Services Project, including a pre-law program, a self-help tutoring program, a dental services program, and a curricula review; an urban affairs workshop; a "Directory of Community Organization"; an "Early Childhood Educational Planning Study"; staff assistance in drawing up proposals for a neighborhood college; an extension center for returning Vietnam veterans; and research into the University Without Walls.

SIX INSTITUTIONS' CONSORTIUM. Ewa U. Eko, Director. Bennett College, 700 Gorrell, Greensboro, North Carolina 27420. 919/275-1907.

Barber-Scotia College, Concord; Bennett College, Greensboro; Livingstone College, Salisbury; Saint Augustine's College, Raleigh; Shaw University, Raleigh; Winston-Salem State University, Winston-Salem; all of North Carolina.

Cooperation within the Consortium is directed toward curriculum and faculty development, African and Afro-American Studies and cultural enrichment, developmental education, and the improvement of counseling and student personnel services. Program support and opportunities are also given to the improvement of library staff and material resources, the effective utilization of institutional personnel and expertise, and the sharing of lyceum and cultural activities. New and projected programs include academic management development and faculty student travel seminars to West Africa.

SOUTH CAROLINA FOUNDATION OF INDEPENDENT COLLEGES, INC. J. Lacy McLean, Executive Vice-President. 1110 Daniel Building, Greenville, South Carolina 29602. 803/233-6894.

Coker College, Hartsville; Columbia College, Columbia; Converse College, Spartanburg; Erskine College, Due West; Furman University, Greenville; Limestone College, Gaffney; Newberry College, Newberry; Presbyterian College, Clinton; Wofford College, Spartanburg.

Each program is run as a separate consortium, with the Foundation acting rather like a holding company. The nine "program consortia" are Corporate Support (nine colleges)—fund raising; South Carolina College Council (sixteen colleges)—governmental relationships; International Education (twelve colleges)—four roving professors, faculty development, visiting lecturers, and a film library; Planning Center (eleven colleges)—workshops, administrative development; Purchasing (nineteen colleges)—joint purchase; Staff Officers Program (twelve colleges)—periodical meetings for planning of joint programs; Visiting Lecturers; Foreign Studies Program; and Tuition Grants Program—administration of state financial program.

SOUTHERN CONSORTIUM FOR INTERNATIONAL EDUCATION, INC. C. C. Murray, Executive Director. Georgia Center for Continuing Education, Room 241, University of Georgia, Athens, Georgia 30601. 404/542-4048.

Atlanta University, Atlanta; Emory University, Atlanta; Georgia Institute of Technology, Atlanta; Georgia State University, Atlanta; Medical College of Georgia, Athens; University of Georgia, Athens; Georgia Southern College, Statesboro; all of Georgia.

scie was organized and incorporated to conduct programs of international research, teaching, and service among its member institutions and between them and the world community. The major thrust of scie is to provide opportunities for its scholars to become better acquainted with world society through involvement in international affairs.

SOUTHWEST ALLIANCE FOR LATIN AMERICA. R. H. Hancock, Executive Director. 1700 Asp Avenue, Norman, Oklahoma 73069. 405/325-1751.

Arizona State University, Tempe; Baylor University, Waco, Texas; Kansas State University, Manhattan; Louisiana Technical University, Ruston; New Mexico State University, Las Cruces; North Texas State University, Denton; Oklahoma City University, Oklahoma City; Southwest Texas State University, San Marcos; Texas A & I University, Kingsville; Texas Technical University, Lubbock; University of Colorado, Boulder; University of Denver, Denver; University of Oklahoma, Norman; University of Tulsa, Tulsa.

sala was formed to improve university involvement in the life and culture of Latin America and to institutionalize service in Latin American programs as an integral part of a faculty. sala has functioned as a technical assistance contracting organization, but looks for activities in a broader Latin American field. sala is considering a program to move the emphasis away from the training of specialists to the training of nonspecialists—laymen or professional practitioners in business, education, health, agriculture, home economics, engineering, and the sciences. sala is also formulating programs to improve and facilitate the training of Latin Americans at sala institutions on the home campus or at Latin American centers.

SUNY 4 CENTER. Yole de Blasio, Executive Director. State University of New York, 60 East 42 Street, New York, New York 10017. 212/687-6681.

Agricultural and Technical College at Farmingdale; Borough of Manhattan Community College, New York; Bronx Community College, New York; Dutchess Community College, Poughkeepsie; Empire State College, Saratoga Springs; Fashion Institute of Technology, New York; Fiorello H. LaGuardia Community College, Long Island

City; Hostos Community College, New York; Kingsborough Community College, Brooklyn; Long Island Learning Center, Old Westbury; Manhattan Learning Center, New York; Nassau Community College, Garden City; New York City Community College, Brooklyn; Orange County Community College, Middletown; Queensborough Community College, Bayside; Rockland Community College, Suffern; State University of New York Downstate Medical Center, Brooklyn; State University at Stony Brook; State University College at New Paltz; State University College at Old Westbury; State University College at Purchase; State University College of Optometry, New York; State University Maritime College, New York; Staten Island Community College; Suffolk County Community College, Selden; Sullivan County Community College, South Fallsburgh; Ulster County Community College, Stone Ridge; Westchester Community College, Valhalla.

SUNY 4 Center serves as an information center on education opportunities available in the State University of New York generally and, more specifically, in Coordinating Area number four; as a coordinating center and physical base location for the State University seminars in New York City; as a coordinating office and clearinghouse for regional use of the university Scholar Exchange Program; as a coordinating center for the proposed *Semester in New York* program of the State University; as a regional coordinating center for cultural programs; and as a communication link with the staff of the City University of New York and other New York City educational institutions.

THE ASSOCIATION FOR GRADUATE EDUCATION AND RESEARCH OF NORTH TEXAS. Ross C. Peavey, Executive Director. P.O. Box 30365, Dallas, Texas 75230. 214/231-7211.

Participant institutions: Southern Methodist University, Dallas; Texas Christian University, Fort Worth; University of Dallas, Irving; University of Texas at Dallas; University of Texas Southwestern Medical School, Dallas. Associate participant institutions: Austin College, Sherman; Bishop College, Dallas; Dallas Baptist College; Texas Wesleyan College, Fort Worth.

TAGER has a closed-circuit television system, with on-campus studio-originating classrooms and receiving classrooms, two-way interconnection facilities, and receiving classrooms in industrial plants.

TEXAS ASSOCIATION OF DEVELOPING COLLEGES, INC. Walter B. Johnson, Executive Director. B-116 Braniff Tower, Dallas, Texas 75235. 214/358-1591.

Bishop College, Dallas; Huston-Tillotson College, Austin; Jarvis Christian College, Hawkins; Paul Quinn College, Waco; Texas College, Tyler; Wiley College, Marshall.

TADC programs include strengthening departments of business administration through restructuring these departments, through exchange of professors and grants for employment of professors, and through developing common core curriculums; running a cooperative admissions program; training administrative and support personnel in member colleges; and training trustees of the colleges for more effective trusteeship.

TRIANGLE ASSOCIATION OF COLLEGES OF SOUTH CAROLINA AND GEORGIA, INC. Paula Liggins, Acting Executive Director. Middleburg Office Mall, Suite 208, 2700 Middleburg Drive, Columbia, South Carolina 29204. 803/779-4783.

Allen University, Columbia, South Carolina; Benedict College, Columbia, South Carolina; Claflin College, Orangeburg, South Carolina; Morris College, Sumter, South Carolina; Paine College, Augusta, Georgia; Voorhees College, Denmark, South Carolina.

The Association operates an in service training program to develop skills of personnel involved in the area of student services; an interlibrary cooperative program for the joint purchasing and joint processing of books; an inservice training program for paraprofessional library workers; and a cooperative lyceum of visiting scholars, lecturers, and other persons of note.

TRI-COLLEGE UNIVERSITY, INC. Albert Anderson, Coordinating Provost. 321 N. 4th Street (P.O. Box 2443), Fargo, North Dakota 58102. 701/237-5041.

Concordia College, Moorhead, Minnesota; Moorhead State College, North Dakota State University, Fargo.

The Tri-College University is in a three-year development supported by the National Endowment for the Humanities to upgrade programs on the campuses in conjunction with the Humanities Forum, a joint center for the multidisciplinary study of the humanities. In addition to cross-registration and course exchange under varying agreements, members of Tri-College have a completely coordinated library system (including daily interlibrary shuttle service, teletype referral, and a computerized union list of periodicals) and intercampus transportation.

TWELVE COLLEGE EXCHANGE.   Philip Driscoll, Executive Director. Two Hebe Court, Norton, Massachusetts 02766. 617/285-7110.

Amherst College, Amherst, Massachusetts; Bowdoin College, Brunswick, Maine; Connecticut College, New London, Connecticut; Dartmouth College, Hanover, New Hampshire; Mount Holyoke College, South Hadley, Massachusetts; Smith College, Northampton, Massachusetts; Trinity College, Hartford, Connecticut; Vassar College, Poughkeepsie, New York; Wellesley College, Wellesley, Massachusetts; Wesleyan University, Middletown, Connecticut; Wheaton College, Norton, Massachusetts; Williams College, Williamstown, Massachusetts.

The primary function of the Twelve College Exchange has been the exchange of students from one campus to another for a semester or year in residence. A number of other projects have been under consideration, among them a National Theater Institute involving Connecticut College, the Eugene O'Neill Memorial Theater Center, and the Twelve College Exchange for student internship in drama, a Taiwan-Hong Kong Year Abroad Program initiated by Wellesley College, and possibilities of establishing joint urban centers in Boston and Washington.

TWIN CITIES INTER-COLLEGE COOPERATION.   Andrew E. Helmich, Director. Office of Inter-College Cooperation, 122 O'Shaughnessy Educational Center, College of St. Thomas, St. Paul, Minnesota 55105. 612/647-5228.

Augsburg College, Minneapolis; Hamline University, St. Paul; Macalester College, St. Paul; College of St. Catherine, St. Paul; College of St. Thomas, St. Paul.

Twin Cities Inter-College Cooperation has cooperative programs in admissions, transportation for cross-registration, urban affairs, minority education, and general joint developmental efforts.

UNION FOR EXPERIMENTING COLLEGES AND UNIVERSITIES.   Samuel Baskin, President. Antioch College, Yellow Springs, Ohio 45387. 513/767-7331.

Antioch College, Yellow Springs, Ohio; Bard College, Annandale-on-Hudson, New York; Chicago State College; Friends World College, Westbury, New York; Goddard College, Plainfield, Vermont;

Hofstra University, Hempstead, New York; Loretto Heights College, Denver, Colorado; Northeast Illinois State College, Chicago; Roger Williams College, Bristol, Rhode Island; Staten Island Community College, New York; Stephens College, Columbia, Missouri; University of Massachusetts, Amherst; University of Minnesota, Minneapolis; University of the Pacific, Stockton, California; University of Wisconsin at Green Bay; Westminster College, Fulton, Missouri.

The Union for Experimenting Colleges and Universities at Antioch College has an unconventional program in higher education, University Without Walls, which is designed to make college-level education more flexible and available to persons of all ages from sixteen to sixty and over.

UNION OF INDEPENDENT COLLEGES OF ART. Dean E. Tollefson, Executive Director. 4340 Oak Street, Kansas City, Missouri 64111. 816/ 753-8238.

California College of Arts and Crafts, Oakland; Cleveland Institute of Art, Cleveland, Ohio; Kansas City Art Institute, Kansas City, Missouri; Maryland Institute, College of Art, Baltimore; Minneapolis College of Art and Design, Minneapolis, Minnesota; Philadelphia College of Art, Philadelphia, Pennsylvania; Rhode Island School of Design, Providence; San Francisco Art Institute, San Francisco, California.

UICA programs include cooperative support for curriculum development; summer grants for individual faculty; faculty and student intercampus work; a joint-use film center; exchange of library resources; cooperative admissions work including the Mutual Application Plan; and deans, business and development officers projects; a student mobility program, which allows students enrolled at any one of the member colleges to arrange a program of study for one or two semesters at another member college; a transfer program available in most instances to students completing the freshman year in good standing at one UICA member institution who wish to transfer to another member institution without loss of credit or time; and a junior year abroad program for study in Mexico, Italy, and England. Other cooperative programs exist in such areas as faculty exchange, curricular development, and library resources.

UNITED COLLEGES OF SAN ANTONIO. William G. Kelly, Executive Director. 300 W. Woodlawn, San Antonio, Texas 78212. 512/735-5281.

Incarnate Word College, Oblate College of the Southwest, Our Lady of the Lake College. St. Mary's University.

UCSA is engaged in a major interinstitutional planning project; student and faculty interchange; an ethnic studies program; a cooperative counseling program; and a marketing survey for the institutions.

UNIVERSITY CENTER AT HARRISBURG.   Robert A. Byerly, Director. 2991 North Front Street, Harrisburg, Pennsylvania 17110. 717/238-9694.

Elizabethtown College, Elizabethtown; Lebanon Valley College, Annville; Pennsylvania State University, University Park; Temple University, Philadelphia; University of Pennsylvania, Philadelphia.

The cooperating institutions of the University Center at Harrisburg have uniform tuition rates, mutual exchange of credits, and share faculty and administrative personnel. The basic function of the Center is to supply a means of bringing to Harrisburg area college educational programs, at the undergraduate and graduate levels, designed to meet the academic, vocational, and cultural needs of persons in Central Pennsylvania.

UNIVERSITY CENTER IN GEORGIA, INC.   Richard K. Murdoch, Director. Lustrat House, University of Georgia, Athens, Georgia 30601. 404/542-3715.

Agnes Scott College, Decatur; Atlanta School of Art; Atlanta University Center; Columbia Theological Seminary, Decatur; Emory University, Atlanta; Georgia Institute of Technology, Atlanta; Georgia State University, Atlanta; Oglethorpe College, Atlanta; University of Georgia, Athens.

The purpose of the University Center in Georgia is to promote and develop cooperative and coordinated educational and research programs in participating institutions.

UNIVERSITY CENTER IN VIRGINIA, INC.   W. Donald Rhinesmith, President. Jefferson Hotel, Jefferson and Main Streets, Richmond, Virginia 23220. 703/644-1093.

Bridgewater College, Bridgewater; College of William and Mary, Williamsburg; Hampden-Sydney College, Hampden-Sydney; Hampton Institute, Hampton; Longwood College, Farmville; Madison College, Independent City; Mary Baldwin College, Staunton; Mary Washington College, Fredericksburg; Presbyterian School of Christian Education, Richmond; Radford College, Radford; Randolph-Macon

College, Ashland; Randolph-Macon Woman's College, Lynchburg; Roanoke College, Salem; Saint Paul's College, Lawrenceville; Sweet Briar College, Sweet Briar; Union Theological Seminary, Richmond, University of Richmond, Richmond; University of Virginia, Charlottesville; Virginia Commonwealth University, Richmond; Virginia Military Institute, Lexington; Virginia State College, Petersburg; Virginia Union University, Richmond; Washington and Lee University, Lexington.

Among the programs run by the University Center in Virginia, are visiting scholars; two workshop studies in the International City of the Arts in Paris; cooperative purchasing of science laboratory apparatus and supplies and library books; and a film library.

WESTERN KANSAS COMMUNITY SERVICES CONSORTIUM. Karen Pollock, Executive Director. Dodge City Community College, 14th and HiWay 50 By-Pass, Dodge City, Kansas 67801. 316/225-1312, ext. 218.

Cloud County Community College, Concordia; Colby Community College, Colby; Dodge City Community College, Dodge City; Garden City Community College, Garden City; Hutchinson Community College, Hutchinson; Pratt County Community College, Pratt; Seward County Community College, Liberal.

The Western Kansas Community Services Consortium is mainly a means of providing cooperative, unified efforts to solve community problems for western Kansas. It offers programs in cultural arts and the humanities and serves as a clearinghouse for ideas, programs, projects, and financial assistance for community services.

WORCESTER CONSORTIUM FOR HIGHER EDUCATION, INC. Lawrence E. Fox, Executive Director. Boynton Hall, Worcester Polytechnic Institute, Worcester, Massachusetts 01609. 617/753-1411.

Anna Maria College, Paxton; Assumption College, Worcester; Becker Junior College, Worcester; Clark University, Worcester; College of the Holy Cross, Worcester; Leicester Junior College, Leicester; Quinsigamond Community College, Worcester; University of Massachusetts Medical School, Worcester; Worcester Junior College; Worcester Polytechnic Institute; Worcester State College. Associate members: American Antiquarian Society, Worcester; Crafts Center, Worcester; International Center of Worcester; Old Sturbridge Village, Sturbridge; Worcester Art Museum; Worcester Foundation for Experimental Biology, Shrewsbury; Worcester Historian Society; Worcester Horticultural Society; Worcester Science Center.

Among Worcester Consortium programs are activities in the following areas: making available class lists of courses registering ten or fewer students to the academic deans; consideration of joint emergency psychiatric services by the student personnel deans; cooperation by business officers in such areas as ice rinks, sports facilities, and hiring the disadvantaged; joint purchasing of such items as fuel oil, paper products, chemicals, landscape materials, and cleaning materials; and operating three shuttle buses. Other major activities include the Management of Health Enterprises Option, utilizing the collective courses of the institutions in organized health care and related activities, no-charge cross-registration, and library cooperation featuring an Inter-Library Book Shuttle and an Inter-Library Teletype System.

BIBLIOGRAPHY

ANDREWS, W. W. *Cooperation Within American Higher Education.* Washington, D.C.: Association of American Colleges, 1964.

ANZALONE, J. S. *An Interinstitutional Admissions Program for the State University System of Florida.* Tallahassee, Fla., State University System of Florida, 1967.

Associated Colleges of the Midwest. *ACM: Associated Colleges of the Midwest Faculty Handbook 1970–71.* Chicago, 1970.

Boston Globe. October 31, 1971.

BRADLEY, A. P. "Academic Consortium Effectiveness: An Investigation of Criteria." Ph.D. dissertation, University of Michigan, 1971.

BRENEMAN, D. W. "Selected Aspects of the Economics of the Five College Cooperation." Mimeographed. Amherst, Mass.: Amherst College, 1971.

BURNETT, H. J. (Ed.) *Interinstitutional Cooperation in Higher Education.* Corning, N. Y.: College Center of the Finger Lakes, 1970.

Carnegie Commission on Higher Education. *The More Effective Use of Resources: An Imperative for Higher Education.* New York: McGraw-Hill, 1972.

CASS, J. M. "Changes in American Education in the Next Decade: Some Predictions." In M. B. MILES (Ed.), *Innovation in Edu-*

cation. New York: Columbia University, Teachers College Press, 1964.

Central Steering Committee of the CCFL Self-Study and Long-Range Plan. *Patterns for Voluntary Cooperation: Self-Study Report of the College Center of the Finger Lakes*. Corning, N. Y.: College Center of the Finger Lakes, 1971.

Circular Letter No. 19. Executive Director of the National Association of State Universities and Land-Grant Colleges to Heads of State Universities and Land-Grant Institutions. December 11, 1972.

Council of the Claremont Colleges. *Constitution of The Claremont Colleges (The)*. Claremont, Calif., 1970.

"Criteria for Judging Proposals Submitted Under House Bill 4528: Education Cooperation Act." Mimeographed. Springfield, Ill.: Board of Higher Education, 1972.

DONOVAN, G. F. (Ed.) *College and University Interinstitutional Cooperation*. Washington, D.C.: Catholic University of America Press, 1965.

DUNHAM, E. A. Letter to Franklin Patterson. May 9, 1973.

Education Cooperation Act. Illinois Legislature, 1972.

EKO, E. U. "Voluntary Academic Consortia: The Impact of Multiple Memberships on Private Colleges and Universities." Ph.D. dissertation, Union of Experimenting Colleges and Universities, 1972.

Five College Long-Range Planning Committee. *Five College Cooperation: Directions for the Future*. Amherst, Mass.: University of Massachusetts Press, 1969.

FOX, L. E. "Putting Cooperation into Purchasing Yields Savings." *College and University Business*, 1972, *53* (2).

FREDERICK, E., and OOSTDAM, B. L. (Comps.). *Directory: The Marine Science Consortium, Inc*. Millersville, Pa.: Millersville State College, 1972.

Forest and Range Research News. Press release. February 15, 1972.

GARDNER, J. W. "Agenda for the Colleges and Universities." Mimeographed. San Francisco: California Conference on Higher Education, May 1965.

GRANBERG, L. I. Memorandum to the CMA Committee on Objectives. Orange City, Ia., April 5, 1972.

GRUPE, F. H. "The Establishment of Collegiate Cooperative Centers." Ph.D. dissertation, State University of New York, 1969.

HALVERSON, W. "Early Attempts at Cooperation Among Member Col-

leges of Colleges of Mid-America, Incorporated." Mimeographed. Sioux City, Ia.: Colleges of Mid-America, 1972.

HODGKINSON, H. L. "Impact of Consortia on Institutional Vitality."
Mimeographed. Berkeley: Center for Research and Development in Higher Education, 1972.

JOHNSON, E. L. "Consortia in Higher Education." *Educational Record,*
Fall, 1967.

JORDAN, M. A. "The Functions of the Forces of Autonomy, Cooperative
Interdependence and Conflict in Two Confederations of Higher
Education." Ph.D. dissertation, University of Notre Dame, 1970.

Kansas City Regional Council for Higher Education, "Kansas City
Regional Council for Higher Education." Flyer. Kansas City,
Mo., n.d.

Kansas City Regional Council for Higher Education, KCRCHE *Activities in Brief.* Kansas City, Mo., 1971.

*Kansas City Regional Council for Higher Education—Kansas City,
Missouri.* Typescript. Kansas City, Missouri: Johnson and
Fleet, Certified Public Accountants, 1971.

KELLY, W. G. "The Consortium and the Developing College: A Work-
paper." Mimeographed. Baltimore: Loyola College, n.d.

KILLIAN, J. R., JR. Letter to Franklin Patterson. March 29, 1972.

LANCASTER, R. B. "Interdependency and Conflict in a Consortium for
Cooperation in Higher Education: Toward a Theory of Inter-
organizational Behavior." Ph.D. dissertation, University of Michigan, 1969.

LANIER, W. Letter to Franklin Patterson. January 4, 1972.

MARKUS, F. W. (*Ed.*) *Partners for Education Progress* (PEP). Kansas
City, Mo.: Metropolitan School Study Group, 1967.

MC CAMBRIDGE, R. H. Letter to Franklin Patterson. July 6, 1973.

MILLARD, R. M. "Consortia and Statewide Systems: Complementation
or Chaos?" Address to the Academic Consortium Seminar.
Miami: 1972.

MOORE, R. S. *Consortiums in American Higher Education 1965–66.*
Washington, D.C.: U.S. Department of Health, Education, and
Welfare, 1968. HE 000 160.

MUNROE, H. W. "A Community of Colleges." Mimeographed. Manchester, N. H.: New Hampshire College and University Council,
1971a.

MUNROE, H. W. Letter to Franklin Patterson. December 28, 1971b.

MYERS, J. H. Memorandum to Lawrence Woodworth. Washington,
D.C., August 16, 1972.

NELSEN, W. C. *Entrepreneurship and Innovation in Consortia.* St. Louis, Mo.: Danforth Foundation, 1972a.

NELSEN, W. C. (Ed.) *Higher Education Consortia: Idea of the Past or Wave of the Future?* St. Louis, Mo.: Danforth Foundation, 1972b.

New York *Times.* September 28, 1971.

Oak Ridge Associated Universities. "Twenty-fifth Annual Report." Oak Ridge, Tenn. 1971.

PALTRIDGE, J. G. *Urban Higher Education Consortia.* Berkeley: Center for Research and Development in Higher Education, 1971.

"Papers of the Twenty-fifth Meeting of the ACM Board of Directors." Mimeographed. Galesburg, Ill.: Knox College, 1972.

PARKINSON, R. D. "Selected Voluntary Academic Consortia in Higher Education: Financial Aspects." Ph.D. dissertation, University of Indiana, 1972.

PATTERSON, F. K. "The Consortium Movement: Fad or Forecast?" *World,* July 1972, 2.

PATTERSON, F. K., and LONGSWORTH, C. R. *The Making of a College.* Cambridge, Mass.: MIT Press, 1966.

PATTERSON, L. D. "A Descriptive Study of the Governance of Selected Voluntary Academic Cooperative Arrangements in Higher Education." Ph.D dissertation, Kansas City, University of Missouri, 1971a.

PATTERSON, L. D. *Consortia in American Higher Education.* Washington, D.C.: ERIC Clearinghouse on Higher Education, November 1970.

PATTERSON, L. D. "The Potential of Consortia." *Compact,* October 1971b, 5 (5).

PATTERSON, L. D. (Ed.) *Comprehensive Bibliography on Interinstitutional Cooperation with Special Emphasis on Voluntary Academic Consortia in Higher Education.* Kansas City, Mo.: Kansas City Regional Council for Higher Education, 1971c.

PATTERSON, L. D. (Ed.) *Consortium Directory: Voluntary Academic Cooperative Arrangements in Higher Education.* 5th ed. Kansas City, Mo.: Kansas City Regional Council for Higher Education, 1971d.

PATTERSON, L. D. (Ed.) *Papers of the Academic Consortium Seminar.* Vol. 7. Kansas City, Mo.: Kansas City Regional Council for Higher Education, 1972.

Piedmont University Center. "Piedmont University Center, May 2, 1972." Mimeographed. Winston-Salem, N. C., 1972.

PROVO, T. L. "A Change Process Model for Bilateral Interinstitutional Cooperation in Higher Education." Ph.D. dissertation, Kansas State University, 1971.

SAGAN, E. L. "A Network Model of Steps for the Implementation of the Planning and Establishing of Higher Education Consortiums." Ph.D. dissertation, Ohio State University, 1969.

SALERNO, M. D. *Patterns of Interinstitutional Cooperation in American Catholic Higher Education—1964.* Washington, D.C.: Catholic University of America Press, 1966.

SCHWENKMEYER, B., and GOODMAN, M. E. *Putting Cooperation to Work.* New York: Academy for Educational Development, 1972.

SILVERMAN, R. J. "Toward an Inter-Organizational Theory in Higher Education." Ph.D. dissertation, Cornell University, 1969.

SMITH, A. K. Letter to Franklin Patterson. May 28, 1973.

SWERDLOW, K. G. "Selected Voluntary Academic Consortia in Higher Education: Academic Program." Ph.D. dissertation, University of Indiana, 1972.

TOLLEFSON, D. E. Letter to Franklin Patterson. January 4, 1972.

TRENDLER, C. A. "Interinstitutional Cooperation for Academic Development Among Small Church-Related Liberal Arts Colleges." Unpublished doctoral dissertation. Indiana University, Bloomington, 1967.

TROUT, W. E. "The Kentuckiana Metroversity: Case Study of a Consortium." Master's thesis, University of Louisville, 1972.

WALKER, E. L. "Report of the President." Mimeographed. Sioux Falls, S. D., 1972.

WELLS, R. V. "Prolegomenon to Any Redefinition of CMA Goals." Mimeographed. Sioux Falls, S. D., 1972.

WILSON, L. (Ed.) *Emerging Patterns in American Higher Education.* Washington, D.C.: American Council on Education, 1965.

WITTICH, J. J. (Ed.) *College and University Interinstitutional Cooperation.* Corning, N. Y.: College Center of the Finger Lakes, 1962.

ZIMMERMAN, W. D. "A Foundation Executive's Assessment of the College Consortia Movement." In L. D. PATTERSON (Ed.), *Papers of the Academic Consortia Seminar on Assessing the Consortium Movement.* Mimeographed. Kansas City, Mo.: Kansas City Regional Council for Higher Education, 1968.

INDEX